The Bullmastiff: Guardian and Gentle Giant

RUI NAVARRO

Copyright © 2023 Rui Navarro

All rights reserved.

ISBN: 9798399934556

ps, for example) were introduced to improve his lines.

THE BULLMASTIFF

Chapter 1: Introduction to the Bullmastiff ------------7

Chapter 2: Physical Traits of the Bullmastiff ---------22

Chapter 3: Personality and Temperament -------------38

Chapter 4: Bullmastiffs and Health--------------------56

Point 7: Signs of a Healthy Bullmastiff ---------------75

Chapter 5: Nutrition Needs----------------------------79

Chapter 6: Training Essentials-------------------------99

Chapter 7: Exercise and Mental Stimulation --------124

Chapter 8: Grooming Your Bullmastiff --------------147

Chapter 9: Breeding and Genetics --------------------167

Chapter 10: Bullmastiffs and Legislation-------------189

Chapter 11: Bullmastiffs in Work and Sports -------210

Chapter 12: Life with a Bullmastiff ------------------229

Conclusion: Is a Bullmastiff Right for You? --------249

ABOUT THE AUTHOR -----------------------------254

THE BULLMASTIFF

Copyright © 2023 by Rui Navarro

All rights reserved. No part of this book may be reproduced in any form or by any electronic or mechanical means, including information storage and retrieval systems, without permission in writing from the publisher, except by a reviewer who may quote brief passages in a review.

The information in this book is true and complete to the best of the author's knowledge. All recommendations are made without guarantee on the part of the author or publisher. The author and publisher disclaim any liability in connection with the use of this information.

This book is intended for informational purposes only. The author and publisher shall not be liable for any loss or damage caused or alleged to be caused directly or indirectly by the information contained in this book.

Published by Rui Navarro

Book design by Rui Navarro

First Edition, 2023

THE BULLMASTIFF

CHAPTER 1: INTRODUCTION TO THE BULLMASTIFF

Welcome, dear reader, to our journey through the world of the Bullmastiff, a breed known as both a guardian and a gentle giant. This is a breed that's packed with personality, wrapped in a burly and commanding presence.

The Bullmastiff has a history rich with purpose and duty. They were originally bred in the United Kingdom back in the 19th century. The aim was to create a robust dog breed that could guard estates and ward off poachers. Combining the strength of the Mastiff and the tenacity of the Bulldog, the Bullmastiff was designed for resilience, courage, and reliability.

The Bullmastiff is a breed that is both commanding and loving, balancing its historical role as a protector with its modern role as a family companion. Today, these dogs are known as fearless family protectors and, at the same time, affectionate companions who are genuinely gentle with those they love.

But how popular is this breed? Well, while they might not be the first breed that comes to mind when people think about getting a dog, Bullmastiffs have a steady and dedicated following. According to the American Kennel Club's popularity ranking, as of my knowledge cut-off in September 2021, Bullmastiffs were placed as the 51st most popular breed in the United States. This shows they have a firm paw print in the hearts of many dog lovers.

There's something unique about Bullmastiffs that sets them apart from other breeds. They're not just big dogs; they're dogs with big hearts, and even bigger personalities. Their eyes speak volumes, conveying emotions that range from resolute determination when on guard, to soulful affection when they nuzzle up to their favorite humans. These dogs have a dignified aura about them, a quality that commands respect and adoration.

In this book, we'll journey together through the world of the Bullmastiff, exploring everything from their history, physical traits, and temperament to their health, nutritional needs, and beyond. Whether you're a prospective Bullmastiff owner or a seasoned guardian of this incredible breed, there's something in this book for you.

Our journey will also include chapters on the essentials of training, their need for exercise and mental stimulation, grooming, and the all-important subject of their health. We'll dive into the importance of responsible breeding and the impact of legislation on this breed.

Lastly, we'll explore the real-life experiences of living with a Bullmastiff, stories from owners, and some necessary conversations about their role in work, sports, and life in general.
So, sit back, get comfortable, and prepare to be immersed in the world of the Bullmastiff, the guardian, and the gentle giant.
Welcome aboard to this journey - let's discover the world of Bullmastiffs together!

History and Origins of the Breed

The history of the Bullmastiff is not just the tale of a dog breed. It's a story of purpose, determination, and the ingenuity of breeders who needed a dog that could protect vast British estates from poachers. Our journey back in time takes us to the 19th century United Kingdom, a time when noble lords, gamekeepers, and estate owners were dealing with a persistent problem.

Poaching was a rampant issue back in the 1800s in England. The vast, sprawling estates were attractive targets for poachers who sought to illegally hunt game from the property. To combat this, estate owners and gamekeepers needed a guard dog. But not just any guard dog would do. They needed a dog that was fast, brave, loyal, and formidable - a dog that could track quietly, attack forcefully, and pin down any intruders without severely injuring them. A delicate balance indeed, between strength and restraint.

In search of this ideal protector, gamekeepers began to selectively breed dogs that would eventually become the Bullmastiff we know today. They turned to the English Mastiff for its size, strength, and courageous spirit, and to the Bulldog for its tenacity, agility, and fearlessness. The breeders sought a mix that was around 60% Mastiff and 40% Bulldog - a blend that would ultimately yield the qualities they desired in their ultimate estate guardian.

By the late 19th century, the Bullmastiff had come into its own as a breed. These dogs were exactly what the gamekeepers had hoped for: large, but not too large to be slow or cumbersome; brave, but not so aggressive as to seriously harm a human; and loyal, always willing to put themselves in harm's way to protect their home and family.

In 1924, the Bullmastiff was officially recognized as a pure breed in England. A few years later, in 1933, the American Kennel Club (AKC) followed suit and recognized the Bullmastiff as a pure breed in the Working Group category.

It's remarkable to consider that the traits bred into the Bullmastiff all those years ago for a very specific purpose - traits like courage, loyalty, strength, and protective instinct - are still an integral part of the breed's identity today. These qualities, originally intended to ward off poachers, are now what make the Bullmastiff such a treasured family pet and protective companion.

From their inception as the gamekeeper's night watchman, Bullmastiffs have come a long way. They've moved from the grounds of sprawling British estates to homes all over the world, where they're cherished not only as protective guardians but also as loving family pets.

They carry their history in their genes, their large and imposing stature a testament to the formidable protectors they once were, their gentle and affectionate nature a sign of their adaptability to a more domesticated role.

That's the beauty of the Bullmastiff's story – it's a rich tapestry of resilience, functionality, and affection. And, as we will see, this history plays a significant role in understanding the Bullmastiff as a breed and as our companion.

General Description of Bullmastiffs

As we turn the page from history to the present, let's now paint a picture of what the Bullmastiff looks like. When you first set eyes on a Bullmastiff, what words spring to mind? Majestic, perhaps? Powerful? These are common reactions, and with good reason!

The Bullmastiff is a large and imposing dog breed. But despite its size, it carries itself with a blend of nobility and approachability that's quite unique. It's almost as if the dog knows it's impressive and enjoys playing the part!

A fully grown Bullmastiff stands tall and proud. The breed's standard height ranges from 24 to 27 inches at the shoulder, with males typically being larger than females. But even with this size, they carry an element of grace and agility in their stride.

One of the breed's most distinctive features is its broad, wrinkled head with a short, wide, and deep muzzle. Their dark eyes, set far apart, glow with intelligence and warmth, often hinting at the dog's mood. Bullmastiffs are often described as having a "keen" expression, a look of alertness and curiosity about the world around them.
Their ears are V-shaped, set high, and wide apart, folding close to their head. The tail is set high, tapering from the base to the tip and reaching the hocks. When the Bullmastiff moves, the tail is carried level with the back.

They have a dense, slightly rough coat that comes in a variety of colors, such as fawn, red, or brindle. Their short, dense fur is weather-resistant, protecting them from cold and wet conditions. And let's not forget about that striking dark mask on their face, which is a characteristic feature of the breed.

The body of a Bullmastiff is well-muscled and powerful, but not bulky. It's a compact power that's all about functional strength, not just show. Every inch of this breed screams efficiency and effectiveness, echoing their history as estate guardians.

The overall impression one gets from a Bullmastiff is of balance, strength, endurance, and alertness. They are not overly exaggerated in any physical attribute, and this balance gives them a harmonious, symmetrical appearance.

But even with this formidable physical presence, the Bullmastiff often surprises people with its gentle demeanor. They're quite the contradiction, these dogs - they can appear tough and intimidating, but are actually full of love and affection for their families.

This is a quick sketch of the Bullmastiff's physical appearance. The breed is a study in contrasts: a powerful body with a gentle soul, a stern gaze filled with love, and a strong, muscular build that houses a heart full of loyalty. As we delve deeper into the Bullmastiff's world, you'll see these contrasts popping up again and again - it's part of what makes the breed so unique and special.

The Purpose of Bullmastiffs in History

As we continue our journey with the Bullmastiff, let's take a moment to appreciate the original role of these dogs and how it shapes their behavior today. Remember, understanding the historical purpose of the breed helps us comprehend why Bullmastiffs behave the way they do and how to fulfill their needs in the present day.

As we mentioned before, Bullmastiffs were initially bred to guard estates in 19th century England. Poaching was a significant problem during this period, with intruders trespassing on large estates to illegally hunt game. The solution? A breed of dog that was big enough to intimidate, brave enough to confront, and controlled enough to subdue without causing severe harm. Enter the Bullmastiff, also known as the 'Gamekeeper's Night Dog.'

The duties of the Bullmastiff were essentially nocturnal. They would patrol the grounds at night with the gamekeeper, their silent strides and dark coats making them nearly invisible in the darkness.

Their excellent sense of smell and acute hearing allowed them to detect intruders. Once they found an intruder, their job was to track, chase, and pin them down without mauling them, waiting for the gamekeeper to arrive.
The qualities bred into the Bullmastiff for these duties were strength, courage, and a certain level of gentleness. Despite their imposing presence, Bullmastiffs were never meant to be attack dogs that caused severe harm. Instead, their role was to apprehend and deter, which meant they needed to be powerful but controlled. This is why Bullmastiffs, even today, are protective yet typically non-aggressive dogs.

With the decline in poaching and the changing nature of work and society, the role of Bullmastiffs began to change. They moved from being outdoor guards to becoming indoor protectors and companions. The qualities that made them excellent guard dogs also made them wonderful family pets.

Today, Bullmastiffs are known for their loyalty, protectiveness, and love for their families. They are often called 'gentle giants' because, despite their size and strength, they are generally calm, gentle, and affectionate with their families, including children.

Their protective instincts make them excellent watchdogs, and their intelligence and willingness to please make them responsive to training.

While their work has changed over time, their sense of duty and protectiveness has not. Bullmastiffs are just as ready to guard their human families as they were to guard sprawling estates in the past. They've adapted to their roles as family pets, but they still carry their history with them, a history that has shaped them into the unique, multi-faceted breed they are today.
It's important for Bullmastiff owners to understand and appreciate their dog's historical purpose. This understanding can help us meet their physical and mental needs, train them more effectively, and deepen our bond with these amazing dogs. After all, knowing where you come from is an essential part of knowing who you are. And for the Bullmastiff, who they are is nothing short of remarkable.

Present-Day Status and Breed Popularity

From the sprawling estates of 19th century England to modern-day homes worldwide, the Bullmastiff has journeyed across time and continents, retaining its unique charm and appeal. Today, the Bullmastiff is recognized not just as a reliable guardian, but also as a cherished member of families around the world.

While they might not be as ubiquitous as some breeds like the Labrador Retriever or the German Shepherd, Bullmastiffs have a loyal following. They're adored for their loyalty, their protective instincts, their gentle nature, and let's not forget, their expressive faces!

As of my knowledge cutoff in September 2021, the Bullmastiff was ranked 51st in breed popularity by the American Kennel Club out of 197 breeds. While that might not place them at the top of the popularity list, it does show that they have a secure and loving place in the hearts of many dog lovers.

Today, Bullmastiffs are recognized by major kennel clubs worldwide, including the American Kennel Club, the United Kennel Club, the Canadian Kennel Club, and The Kennel Club in the UK. This recognition indicates that they meet specific breed standards and are valued for their unique characteristics.

Bullmastiffs are also admired in various dog sports such as obedience, agility, and rally. They might not be the first breed that comes to mind when you think of dog sports, but with the right training and socialization, they can excel in these activities. Participating in these sports is a great way for Bullmastiffs to stay fit, mentally stimulated, and engaged with their owners.

On a different note, their protective instincts and strength also make them valuable in roles such as search and rescue, and therapy work. Their size can be a deterrent in dangerous situations, and their gentle, intuitive nature can provide comfort to those in distress.

When it comes to family homes, the Bullmastiff's adaptability, loyalty, and love for their families make them a wonderful addition. They're particularly known for their patience and gentleness with children, earning them the moniker of 'nanny dogs.' They're also fairly low-energy dogs for their size, meaning they can adapt well to living in smaller spaces as long as they receive adequate exercise.

While it's true that the Bullmastiff may not be the first breed you see in a dog park, their status as the 'gentle guardian' has earned them a special place in the canine world and in the hearts of those lucky enough to share their lives with them. They may not be the most popular breed in numbers, but in the hearts of their owners, they're second to none!

A Brief Overview of the Book

Now that we have a general understanding of the Bullmastiff and its captivating history, I want to give you a little preview of the journey we're about to embark on. This book, dear reader, is your comprehensive guide to all things Bullmastiff, a warm and friendly companion that will help you navigate the diverse world of this unique breed.

As we step forward into the following chapters, we'll be taking a deep dive into the physical traits of the Bullmastiff. We'll explore their impressive size, the variety of their coats, and the strength hidden within their muscular bodies. Every physical detail that makes a Bullmastiff stand out will be put under the microscope, providing a clear and vivid image of this breed's exterior.

But a Bullmastiff is more than just its physical form. So, we'll also be venturing into the rich emotional landscape of this breed, discovering the unique personality traits and temperament that truly make a Bullmastiff, a Bullmastiff. Their interactions with families and children, relationships with other pets, and the role they play as guard dogs - we'll be unraveling these threads one by one.

Health, an integral aspect of any dog's life, will be another focus of our exploration. We'll dive into the common health issues, expected lifespan, the role of regular veterinary check-ups, and the importance of a balanced diet in maintaining a Bullmastiff's health. Speaking of diet, the book will serve up a detailed menu on the Bullmastiff's nutritional needs, from the early puppy stage to the twilight years of their life.

We'll chew on the different types of food suitable for them, discuss weight management, and delve into the impact of nutrition on their overall well-being.
We will journey together into the arena of training, exercise, and mental stimulation, navigating through their unique needs and the best ways to keep a Bullmastiff physically fit and mentally stimulated.

This will be coupled with a foray into the world of grooming, where we'll brush through the essentials of keeping a Bullmastiff looking their best.

Our exploration will then lead us to the intricacies of breeding, genetics, and the significant role they play in the health and character of the breed. Legislation and its impact on Bullmastiffs will also be a crucial checkpoint in our journey, offering insights into breed-specific laws and how to navigate them.

We'll cheer for Bullmastiffs as we explore their involvement in work, sports, and their potential careers. And finally, we'll bring it all home as we talk about the day-to-day realities and joys of sharing your life with a Bullmastiff.

This journey will be rich with detailed information, expert insights, practical tips, and heartfelt stories. It's a book meant not just to educate but to inspire and foster a deeper understanding and appreciation for this wonderful breed. So buckle up and join us as we navigate the exciting, heartwarming, and sometimes challenging world of the Bullmastiff. It's going to be a fascinating ride!

Unique Characteristics That Make Bullmastiffs Stand Out

As we continue on our journey, I want to draw your attention to some of the unique characteristics that make Bullmastiffs truly special. These are the traits that set them apart from the rest of the canine world, the idiosyncrasies that make them, well, Bullmastiffs.

One of the first things you'll notice about a Bullmastiff is their size. They are powerfully built dogs, large and muscular, an embodiment of strength and dignity. But there's a surprising contrast in their gentle demeanor. Despite their formidable size, they are incredibly gentle and affectionate with their families. This combination of power and gentleness is one of the defining traits of the Bullmastiff, a characteristic that makes them such beloved companions.

Their expressive faces are another standout feature. Those dark, observant eyes and that furrowed brow tell a tale of their intelligence and keen observation skills. You'll often find a Bullmastiff watching their surroundings with a thoughtful, discerning gaze, as if contemplating the mysteries of the universe.

Or maybe they're just deciding on their next nap location. Either way, their expressive faces add another layer of depth to their personality. Bullmastiffs are renowned for their loyalty and protective instincts. They were bred to protect, and they take this job very seriously, even today. Whether it's keeping an eye on the kids in the backyard or standing guard at the door when a stranger approaches, a Bullmastiff's protective instinct is always at work. Yet, they're not aggressive dogs.

They're controlled protectors, ready to step in when needed but always measured in their response. Perhaps one of the most endearing characteristics of Bullmastiffs is their love for their families. They're not just pets; they're family members. They thrive on human interaction and companionship and are known to form deep, enduring bonds with their owners.

Living with a Bullmastiff is like having a loyal, lovable, slightly slobbery shadow that follows you around, offering silent support and wet-nosed nudges of affection.

Their adaptability is another aspect that makes them stand out. Bullmastiffs can thrive in both rural and urban environments. Despite their size, they're not overly energetic dogs and can adapt well to apartment living as long as they get their daily dose of exercise.

And let's not forget their bravery. From their origins as estate protectors to their current roles as family guardians, Bullmastiffs are undeniably courageous. They face life and its many challenges with a calm, quiet bravery that's truly admirable.

Each of these traits contributes to the unique charm of the Bullmastiff, making them not just another breed of dog, but a breed apart. They're not just dogs; they're Bullmastiffs, each one a unique mix of strength, loyalty, gentleness, and love. And that, dear readers, is what makes them stand out in the wonderful world of dogs.

CHAPTER 2: PHYSICAL TRAITS OF THE BULLMASTIFF

As we turn the page to our next chapter, let's begin our deeper exploration into the world of the Bullmastiff by focusing on what makes this breed truly distinctive – their physical traits. Like all dog breeds, the Bullmastiff has a unique set of physical characteristics that differentiate them from others, helping them stand out in the crowd. So, buckle up for a closer look at the features that make the Bullmastiff a truly magnificent breed.

The Bullmastiff's build immediately catches the eye. These dogs are substantial in size, powerful and sturdy. They represent the perfect balance between the strength of the Mastiff and the speed of the Bulldog, two breeds from which they originated.

This makes them formidable without being intimidating, powerful without losing their agility. And it's this blend of speed and strength that made them such effective gamekeeper's dogs back in the day.

Let's start with their size. Fully grown male Bullmastiffs typically weigh between 110 to 130 pounds and stand about 25 to 27 inches tall at the shoulder. Females are slightly smaller, usually weighing between 90 to 120 pounds and standing about 24 to 26 inches tall. But don't let their large size fool you. Beneath their hulking exterior, Bullmastiffs are just big softies, gentle and affectionate with their families.

Their coats are another distinguishing feature. Bullmastiffs have a short, dense coat that comes in three colors – fawn, red, and brindle. And while the coat is short, it's also dense and weather-resistant, offering them protection from the elements. This means whether it's a hot summer's day or a chilly winter's morning, your Bullmastiff is well equipped to handle it.

The Bullmastiff's face is full of character. They have a broad, wrinkled head with a short, square muzzle. Their dark hazel eyes are set apart under a furrowed brow, giving them an alert, keen expression. And let's not forget the ears – they're V-shaped and set high and wide apart, folding close to the head. This combination of features results in a face that is expressive, dignified, and undeniably endearing.

Their body is just as impressive. Bullmastiffs have a well-muscled, compact body with a deep, wide chest. The body is powerful, with a straight back and a moderately tucked-up belly, creating a look of strength and agility. The tail is set high and reaches the hock, usually carried straight or curved slightly upwards.

Then there's the matter of puppies versus adults. Bullmastiff puppies are nothing short of adorable. They're chunky, cuddly, and those puppy-dog eyes are sure to melt your heart. But keep in mind, these little furballs grow up to be sizable dogs, so enjoy the puppy stage while it lasts!
Finally, it's worth mentioning how Bullmastiffs compare to similar breeds. They're often confused with Boxers or English Mastiffs due to their similar appearances. But Bullmastiffs have a distinct look, with a stockier build than Boxers and a less massive head than English Mastiffs.

In conclusion, the Bullmastiff's physical traits are a perfect representation of the breed's character – strong yet gentle, dignified yet endearing, powerful yet affectionate. And it's these physical features that make them stand out, adding to the charm of this incredible breed.

As we progress further into this book, we'll see how these traits come into play in their personality, health, and overall life. So, stay with me as we continue to uncover the remarkable world of the Bullmastiff.

Standard Size and Weight

Picture this. You're at a dog park, and you see a variety of breeds running around, playing, chasing balls, and having a good time. Some are small, some medium-sized, and then you spot a larger dog, a truly impressive creature that commands attention without even trying. That, my friend, is likely a Bullmastiff.

Bullmastiffs are undeniably large dogs. But they're not just large; they're powerful and well-proportioned, perfectly balanced in their size and strength. When it comes to their standard size and weight, there are some specific ranges that we need to be aware of. Understanding these can help us better care for our Bullmastiffs, ensuring they're in the optimal range for their health and well-being.

So, how big does a Bullmastiff get? Well, a fully grown male Bullmastiff typically stands about 25 to 27 inches tall at the shoulder, and they weigh in at a substantial 110 to 130 pounds. Imagine, that's nearly the size of a small human! Their size is a testament to their origins, bred to track and hold poachers in 19th-century England. They needed to be large and strong to perform their duties effectively, and boy, do they live up to that!

Females, while slightly smaller, are still quite formidable. They typically stand 24 to 26 inches tall and weigh between 90 and 120 pounds. Though they might be slightly smaller, they're no less impressive. A female Bullmastiff carries herself with the same dignity and strength as her male counterparts, fully living up to the breed's reputation.

Now, if you've got a Bullmastiff pup, keep in mind that they don't start out this large. Bullmastiff puppies are born weighing just about a pound or so, but they grow quickly, and by the time they're about six months old, they can weigh anywhere from 50 to 60 pounds. That's quite a growth spurt! It's like they're on a constant mission to outgrow their puppy bed.

And it's important to remember that, just like humans, every Bullmastiff is unique. Some may be slightly smaller or larger than the standard size and weight. And that's perfectly okay. The key is to ensure they're healthy and well-cared for, no matter their size. Understanding the standard size and weight of a Bullmastiff is more than just knowing the numbers. It's about understanding the space they need, the amount of food you'll need to provide, and the kind of physical activity they require. It's about knowing that your lap dog might soon outgrow your lap but will never outgrow its affection for you.

So, there you have it, the lowdown on the standard size and weight of Bullmastiffs. These magnificent dogs may be big in size, but let me assure you, their hearts are even bigger. Stay tuned as we delve deeper into other physical traits that make this breed truly remarkable.

Description of the Coat and Color

Have you ever seen a painting that captures your attention at first glance? The way the colors blend, the textures interact, and how it all comes together in one beautiful masterpiece? That's what I'm reminded of when I look at the coat of a Bullmastiff. The blend of color, the feel of their coat, it all adds up to one stunning canine masterpiece.

Let's start with the texture of their coat. Bullmastiffs possess a short yet dense double coat. Imagine running your hand down the back of a Bullmastiff.

What you'll feel is a thick, protective outer coat, coupled with a softer, insulating undercoat. This double layer of fur isn't just there to make them feel like a plush toy; it has a purpose. The dense outer layer provides protection from the elements, while the inner layer helps regulate their body temperature, keeping them warm during the colder months and cool during the summer.

Now, let's talk about color. The Bullmastiff's coat is like a painter's palette, featuring shades of fawn, red, and brindle. The fawn is a light, yellowish tan, kind of like the color of wheat in a sunlit field. Then we have the red, which is a rich, deep color, like autumn leaves or a sunset. Last but not least, there's the brindle pattern, a beautiful mosaic of dark stripes on a fawn background, each pattern as unique as a fingerprint.

What's fascinating is the variety in these color shades. You might come across a Bullmastiff with a light fawn coat that's almost cream, while others might sport a darker, reddish-fawn. The red can range from a light red to a deep, rich chestnut. And each brindle Bullmastiff has a unique pattern, making them a one-of-a-kind work of canine art.

But no matter the color of their coat, one thing remains constant – a Bullmastiff's signature 'mask.'

This refers to the darker coloration on their muzzle, often extending up to their eyes. The mask adds depth to their already expressive face and highlights their keen, intelligent eyes.

So, whether your Bullmastiff is a light fawn, a deep red, or a unique brindle, remember that their coat is more than just an aspect of their physical appearance. It's a protective barrier, a heat regulator, and an integral part of their identity.

In the end, a Bullmastiff's coat is like a well-composed symphony. Each note of color and each chord of texture play together in perfect harmony, creating a masterpiece that's beautiful, functional, and uniquely theirs. But remember, as with any masterpiece, it requires the right care and attention, which we will explore later in our grooming chapter. Until then, let's continue our journey exploring the physical traits that make Bullmastiffs the remarkable dogs they are.

Facial Structure and Expression

You know, there's something profoundly endearing about the face of a Bullmastiff. Maybe it's their intelligent eyes, or perhaps it's their expressive eyebrows that seem to portray a depth of emotion beyond what we humans can comprehend. Or, it might just be that distinctive, loving look they reserve for their favorite humans. Whatever it is, the facial structure and expressions of a Bullmastiff have a way of tugging at your heartstrings.

The facial structure of a Bullmastiff is an architectural wonder. These dogs have a broad and deep muzzle that's about one-third the overall length of the head. It's like the sturdy base of a monument, providing a strong foundation for the rest of their facial features. And let's not forget about those pronounced, fleshy flews (that's a fancy term for their lips), which often make it seem like they're on the verge of a thoughtful smile.

Above this sturdy base sit their dark, medium-sized eyes, set far apart and slightly sunken. These eyes, often described as 'hazel' or darker, are one of their most expressive features. They can show you a world of emotions, from joy to curiosity, and sometimes, a hint of their infamous stubbornness. But, most of all, they reflect the breed's inherent good-nature, kindness, and a deep-rooted desire to please their human companions.

Now, perched atop this grand structure are their V-shaped ears. When a Bullmastiff is alert, their ears fold and carry a forward flap, adding a sense of attentiveness to their demeanor. Even when at rest, these ears frame their face in a way that's utterly captivating.

And finally, the centerpiece, the cherry on top if you will, is their distinctive black mask. This darker coloration on their muzzle and around their eyes sets off the rest of their facial features beautifully, adding a sense of mystique and gravitas to their overall appearance.

But these structures are more than just aesthetically pleasing. Each part plays a role in their history. Their strong muzzle harkens back to their days as guard dogs, meant to deter intruders with a single look. Their expressive eyes and ears have been tools of communication, revealing their intentions and emotions to their human companions for generations.

To see a Bullmastiff's face is to look into the heart of the breed. It's a blend of strength and gentleness, of resilience and loyalty, of power and an undeniable charm. And the expressions they wear? Those are mirrors into their unique personalities, each one a testament to their intelligence, their emotional acuity, and their deep connection with their human families. But remember, it's not just about admiring their faces from afar. Understanding their facial structure and expressions can help us communicate with them, understand their needs, and strengthen our bond with these beautiful animals. So the next time you find yourself lost in the gaze of a Bullmastiff, remember, you're not just looking at a face; you're looking at the essence of the breed.

Body Shape and Musculature

When you first lay eyes on a Bullmastiff, it's impossible not to notice their impressive physique. This breed's body shape and musculature are a testament to its history, designed for strength, agility, and an imposing presence. It's like they're the canine version of a seasoned athlete, all muscle and might, yet with an underlying elegance that captivates all who see them.

Bullmastiffs possess a large, robust frame, which can be described as powerfully built yet proportionate. Their body is slightly longer than it is tall, creating a somewhat rectangular silhouette. This shape provides the perfect foundation for their commanding presence, allowing them to move with grace despite their size.

But what truly sets them apart is their remarkable musculature. Imagine the body of a Bullmastiff as a landscape of rolling hills and deep valleys, all molded from solid muscle. Their wide chest, muscular back, and strong legs all contribute to their overall powerful appearance.

Take a closer look at their chest. It's broad and deep, reaching down to their elbows, with a well-sprung ribcage that provides plenty of space for their lungs and heart. This allows for excellent stamina, a quality vital to their historical role as estate guardians. This part of their structure is an essential aspect of their impressive physical prowess, hinting at their innate strength and endurance.

As for their back, it's straight, short, and level, leading to a muscular loin and slightly arched croup. When you see a Bullmastiff in motion, you'll notice how this structure comes into play. It contributes to their agility, ensuring they move with a free, smooth, and powerful gait, a fascinating contrast to their hefty build.

Now, let's talk about their legs. Sturdy, straight, and set well apart, these pillars of strength provide the necessary support for their substantial body. Their front legs are straight and strong, leading to round, well-padded feet. The hind legs, meanwhile, are muscular and well-developed, reflecting the power they bring to their motion.

Yet, within this brawny exterior lies an important message: the essence of the Bullmastiff's nature. Their imposing structure wasn't bred for aggression, but rather for protection and deterrence. Every muscle, every inch of their powerful body speaks to their past, where their mere presence was enough to deter any ill-intentioned trespassers.

Their physical prowess is a testament to their historical roles, and their ability to guard those they care about without resorting to unwarranted aggression.

In the end, the Bullmastiff is an impressive display of canine strength, agility, and elegance, a true embodiment of 'power in tranquility'.

Remember, their physique isn't just about aesthetic appeal, but a physical manifestation of their temperament and history, adding yet another layer to the rich tapestry that is the Bullmastiff. And as we continue to unravel this tapestry, we'll come to understand and appreciate this breed even more.

Bullmastiff Puppies vs. Adults

Whether it's the sight of an adorable Bullmastiff puppy bounding with youthful energy or the quiet, steady presence of a fully-grown adult, each life stage of this breed brings its own unique charm and appeal.

It's like watching the story of a Bullmastiff unfold right before your eyes, each chapter filled with growth, changes, and endless love.

From the moment a Bullmastiff puppy is born, you'll find yourself smitten. They are little bundles of joy, typically weighing around a pound at birth, but don't let their size fool you.

These puppies are born with an abundance of energy and curiosity. They're like tiny explorers setting off on an adventure, eager to discover and make sense of the world around them.

At this stage, they are relatively round, with soft coats and the beginnings of what will eventually develop into their powerful physiques.
As Bullmastiff puppies grow, they transition through a delightful, if not slightly awkward, 'puppy' stage.

Their feet may seem too big for their bodies, and they might seem a little clumsy, but this is all part of their charm. It's during this period that they start to fill out, slowly taking on the characteristic muscular build of their breed.

By the time they reach around six months, their growth becomes more noticeable. They develop a significant increase in both weight and height, as they start to lose their puppy fat and begin to look more like the adult Bullmastiffs they're destined to become.

However, their development is not just physical; they are also learning about the world, from understanding basic commands to developing social skills. It's a stage of immense growth and learning.

Eventually, by the time they are around two to three years old, Bullmastiffs reach adulthood. Now they stand tall and proud, embodying the strength and grace that is so characteristic of their breed. They typically weigh anywhere between 100 to 130 pounds and stand 24 to 27 inches at the shoulder. Their coats have settled into their definitive color, and their muscles are well-developed, giving them their distinctive, powerful appearance.

But it's not just their physical changes that capture the heart. An adult Bullmastiff is a magnificent blend of strength, loyalty, and a gentleness that contradicts their imposing size. The playful, explorative puppy has grown into a protective, reliable companion, displaying the unique blend of tenacity and affection that Bullmastiffs are known for.

The journey from a Bullmastiff puppy to an adult is a beautiful transition to witness. As they grow, so does their bond with their human companions, providing years of companionship, loyalty, and unyielding love.

So, whether you're watching a Bullmastiff puppy playfully discovering the world or enjoying the quiet company of an adult, remember to cherish each moment. After all, each stage of their life offers its own special charm, contributing to the remarkable journey of being a part of a Bullmastiff's life.

Comparison of Bullmastiffs with Similar Breeds

In the vast world of dog breeds, it's common to come across breeds that share certain similarities. One such breed that often gets compared to the Bullmastiff is the Boxer. Both breeds have a strong presence, muscular bodies, and lovable personalities, but there are distinct differences that set them apart.

Let's start with their size. While both the Bullmastiff and the Boxer are considered large breeds, the Bullmastiff is generally larger and more robust. A fully grown Bullmastiff can weigh anywhere from 110 to 130 pounds, while a Boxer typically ranges between 50 to 70 pounds. The Bullmastiff stands taller at the shoulder, with a height of 24 to 27 inches, compared to the Boxer's height of 21.5 to 25 inches. So, if you're looking for a larger, more substantial companion, the Bullmastiff might be the choice for you.

In terms of appearance, their coats differ as well. The Bullmastiff has a short, dense coat that requires minimal grooming. On the other hand, the Boxer has a shorter coat that is also smooth and easy to care for. Both breeds come in various colors, but the Bullmastiff's range includes fawn, red, and brindle, while the Boxer typically displays a combination of fawn or brindle with white markings.

Temperament-wise, the Bullmastiff and the Boxer have distinct but equally lovable personalities. Bullmastiffs are known for their calm and gentle nature, often described as 'gentle giants.' They have a protective instinct and are known to be excellent family dogs. On the other hand, Boxers are energetic, playful, and full of personality. They are known for their exuberance and boundless energy, making them a lively addition to any household.

Both breeds are great with children, but it's important to note that the Bullmastiff's calm and steady demeanor may make them a bit more patient and tolerant, especially with younger kids. Boxers, while also great with children, may be more energetic and exuberant, so it's essential to teach them appropriate behavior and socialization from an early age.

Exercise requirements vary between the two breeds. Bullmastiffs are generally less energetic and require moderate exercise to keep them fit and healthy. They enjoy leisurely walks and are content with a good romp in the yard. Boxers, on the other hand, have higher energy levels and require more exercise and mental stimulation to keep them engaged. Regular playtime, long walks, and opportunities for interactive games are essential to keep Boxers happy and fulfilled.

Both breeds are loyal and make excellent companions, but their individual characteristics may suit different lifestyles and preferences. If you're looking for a calm, protective, and affectionate companion who doesn't require excessive exercise, the Bullmastiff might be the perfect fit. If you're seeking a playful, energetic, and outgoing breed that thrives on activity and interaction, the Boxer could be the ideal choice.
It's important to note that each dog is an individual, and personality traits can vary within a breed. So, it's essential to spend time with both breeds, interact with them, and learn about their specific needs and temperaments before making a decision.

In the end, the choice between a Bullmastiff and a Boxer boils down to personal preferences, lifestyle, and the unique connection you feel with each breed. Whether you choose the Bullmastiff's calm and gentle nature or the Boxer's playful energy, both breeds have a lot to offer in terms of love, companionship, and joy.

CHAPTER 3: PERSONALITY AND TEMPERAMENT

Ah, the heart and soul of every dog – their personality and temperament. These are the traits that make them unique individuals, shaping the bond they form with their human companions. In the case of Bullmastiffs, their personality and temperament are truly something special. So, let's dive deep into the world of Bullmastiff traits and discover what makes them such extraordinary companions.

First and foremost, Bullmastiffs are known for their calm and gentle nature. They exude an air of tranquility that is both comforting and reassuring. They are not typically a high-strung, hyperactive breed. Instead, they prefer a relaxed and peaceful existence, making them perfect for those seeking a companion with a laid-back attitude towards life.

Their gentle nature extends to their interactions with families and children. Bullmastiffs have a natural affinity for children and are often referred to as gentle giants. They possess an innate understanding of the fragility of little ones, and their patient and tolerant nature make them excellent companions for kids of all ages. Whether it's playing fetch in the yard or curling up for a cozy nap, Bullmastiffs are gentle, loving, and protective with their young human counterparts.

When it comes to their relationship with other pets, Bullmastiffs can be surprisingly adaptable. With proper socialization and introductions, they can live harmoniously alongside other dogs and cats. However, as with any breed, it's important to monitor and supervise their interactions to ensure everyone gets along smoothly. Early socialization and training play a crucial role in shaping their behavior towards other animals.

One of the most striking aspects of a Bullmastiff's personality is their inherent protective instinct. They are natural-born guardians, thanks to their historical role as estate protectors. Bullmastiffs have an uncanny ability to assess situations and determine potential threats.

They are alert and vigilant, always on the lookout for any sign of danger. This makes them excellent watchdogs, as their imposing presence alone can deter potential intruders. However, it's worth noting that their protective nature doesn't make them inherently aggressive. With proper socialization and training, they can distinguish between real threats and everyday situations, reacting calmly and appropriately.

Training plays a vital role in shaping a Bullmastiff's temperament. They are intelligent dogs who respond well to positive reinforcement and gentle guidance. Consistency, patience, and a firm yet kind approach are key when training a Bullmastiff. Their desire to please their owners, combined with their inherent loyalty, makes them eager and willing learners. Proper training not only helps develop good behavior but also enhances the bond between you and your Bullmastiff.

Now, let's address a common misconception about Bullmastiffs – their supposed aggression. While they may have a strong protective instinct, aggression is not a characteristic of their breed. In fact, Bullmastiffs are known for their even-tempered and affectionate nature. They are not prone to unnecessary aggression or hostility towards humans or other animals. However, like any dog, individual temperament can vary, and proper socialization and training from an early age are essential for a well-rounded and balanced Bullmastiff.

So, in summary, the Bullmastiff's personality and temperament are a harmonious blend of calmness, gentleness, protectiveness, and loyalty. They are loving companions who adore their families and are especially great with children. Their protective instincts make them reliable watchdogs, while their intelligent nature and eagerness to please make training a joy.

Remember, a Bullmastiff's temperament is a reflection of their breed's rich history and their innate desire to be by your side, offering love, loyalty, and a steady, unwavering presence throughout your life's journey.

General Temperament of Bullmastiffs

Ah, the Bullmastiff's temperament – it's like the warm embrace of a loyal friend, always there to offer comfort, love, and a sense of security. The general temperament of Bullmastiffs is a beautiful tapestry woven with traits that make them truly special and cherished companions.

At the core of a Bullmastiff's temperament lies a gentle and calm nature. These dogs have a remarkable ability to exude a sense of tranquility that can have a calming effect on those around them. They possess a natural inclination to create a harmonious environment, and their presence alone can bring a sense of peace to their human companions. Bullmastiffs are known for their patience and tolerance, especially with children. They have a remarkable understanding of the vulnerability of little ones and are careful not to exert unnecessary force or excitement during play. Instead, they approach interactions with a gentle and considerate manner, ensuring that both child and dog have a safe and enjoyable experience together.

Another aspect of their general temperament is their loyalty. Bullmastiffs are incredibly devoted to their families. They form deep bonds with their human companions and will go to great lengths to protect and care for them. Their loyalty knows no bounds, and they have a natural instinct to put their loved ones' well-being above their own.

When it comes to strangers, Bullmastiffs can initially be reserved or aloof. However, their cautious nature doesn't stem from aggression or hostility but rather from a desire to assess the situation and ensure the safety of their family. With proper socialization and positive experiences, they can warm up to new people and become accepting of visitors. Still, their protective instincts remain intact, and they will always prioritize the well-being of their loved ones.

While their loyalty and protectiveness shine bright, Bullmastiffs are not typically an overly vocal breed. They tend to be quiet dogs, not prone to excessive barking or unnecessary noise. This calm demeanor contributes to their peaceful presence and makes them well-suited for various living environments, including apartments and family homes.
Part of the Bullmastiff's general temperament is their inherent watchful nature. They possess a keen sense of awareness and have an uncanny ability to detect potential threats. Whether it's a subtle change in the environment or an unfamiliar person approaching, Bullmastiffs remain alert and vigilant, ready to respond if necessary. Their watchful nature, combined with their imposing size, acts as a deterrent, making them excellent watchdogs.

It's essential to understand that while Bullmastiffs have a calm and gentle temperament, they still require proper socialization, training, and guidance. Early socialization, exposure to various people, animals, and environments, helps them become well-rounded individuals. Positive reinforcement training methods that focus on reward-based techniques are highly effective with Bullmastiffs, as they are intelligent dogs eager to please their owners.

In conclusion, the general temperament of Bullmastiffs is a harmonious blend of gentleness, loyalty, protectiveness, and watchfulness. They are loving, patient, and devoted companions who bring a sense of calmness and tranquility to their families. Their inherent nature to protect and their unwavering loyalty make them exceptional guardians, always looking out for their loved ones' well-being. So, open your heart and let a Bullmastiff's gentle temperament fill your life with unwavering love, loyalty, and a sense of peace.

Part 2: Interaction with Families and Children

When it comes to Bullmastiffs and their interaction with families and children, the words that come to mind are warmth, affection, and unwavering devotion. These gentle giants have a natural affinity for family life and thrive on the love and companionship they share with their human counterparts.

Bullmastiffs are renowned for their gentle nature, making them excellent companions for families of all sizes. They have a deep-rooted desire to be a part of the family unit, participating in everyday activities and forming strong bonds with each family member. Their calm and patient demeanor makes them ideal companions for children, as they possess an innate understanding of the delicate nature of little ones.

Children and Bullmastiffs share a unique and magical connection. Their loving and protective instincts shine through when interacting with kids. It's as if they instinctively recognize the vulnerability of children and adjust their behavior accordingly. They are careful not to be rough or boisterous, showing a gentle touch and a sense of playfulness that is perfectly suited for little ones.

Imagine the joy and laughter that fills a room when a Bullmastiff and a child engage in play. The child finds comfort in the Bullmastiff's unwavering presence and steady companionship, while the dog revels in the joy and innocence that children bring. Whether it's a game of fetch in the backyard, a gentle cuddle on the couch, or simply sharing a quiet moment of companionship, the bond between a Bullmastiff and a child is one filled with love, trust, and endless joy. But the relationship between a Bullmastiff and a child goes beyond playtime. Bullmastiffs have a natural protective instinct that extends to their youngest family members. They will stand guard, keeping a watchful eye on children, ensuring their safety and well-being. This innate protective nature is a testament to their deep loyalty and unwavering dedication to their loved ones.

As with any dog-child interaction, supervision is crucial to ensure a safe and harmonious relationship. While Bullmastiffs are known for their patience and gentleness, it's essential to teach children how to properly interact with dogs and respect their boundaries. Teaching children to approach a Bullmastiff calmly, avoid pulling on their ears or tail, and understanding when the dog needs personal space sets the foundation for a positive and lasting bond.

It's worth noting that early socialization and positive experiences are key factors in shaping a Bullmastiff's behavior towards children. Introducing them to various experiences, including encounters with children of different ages, helps them develop positive associations and strengthens their natural affinity for little ones.

The beauty of a Bullmastiff's interaction with families and children lies in the unconditional love and unwavering loyalty they provide. They become an integral part of the family, bringing comfort, joy, and a sense of security to each family member. So, open your home and your heart to a Bullmastiff, and watch as they weave their way into the fabric of your family, creating a bond that will endure a lifetime of cherished memories.

Relationship with Other Pets

In the grand tapestry of family life, our beloved pets often come in pairs or more. And when it comes to Bullmastiffs and their relationship with other pets, the bonds that form are as diverse and heartwarming as the colors of a sunset. Bullmastiffs have the remarkable ability to adapt and coexist with other animals, creating a harmonious and loving environment.

With proper socialization and introductions, Bullmastiffs can live in harmony alongside other dogs and cats. Their gentle nature and calm demeanor allow them to form strong bonds with their furry companions. They approach interactions with a sense of curiosity and understanding, creating a foundation for a peaceful coexistence.

When introducing a Bullmastiff to a new pet, it's important to provide a controlled and gradual introduction. Slowly introduce them in neutral territory, allowing them to become familiar with each other's scents and presence. Supervision is crucial during these initial interactions, ensuring that everyone feels safe and comfortable. With time and positive experiences, Bullmastiffs can forge deep friendships and establish a sense of camaraderie with their animal counterparts.

Bullmastiffs possess a natural inclination for pack dynamics, making them great team players. They understand the concept of hierarchy and respect boundaries, which contributes to their ability to get along with other animals. While their size may be imposing, their gentle and tolerant nature allows them to adapt to different personalities and temperaments, whether it's a playful and energetic dog or a more reserved and independent feline.

When it comes to their interaction with other dogs, Bullmastiffs typically exhibit a friendly and accepting attitude. They are not prone to aggressive behavior or unnecessary dominance. Instead, they approach their four-legged friends with a sense of camaraderie and a willingness to engage in playful interactions. Their large stature and calm disposition often make them the 'gentle giant' of the dog park, leaving a lasting impression on both humans and other canines.

When it comes to cats and other small pets, Bullmastiffs can surprise you with their gentle and respectful nature. With proper introductions and gradual acclimatization, they can learn to coexist peacefully. However, it's important to remember that individual temperaments and personalities can vary, both in Bullmastiffs and other animals. Some Bullmastiffs may have a higher prey drive or may require additional time and training to adapt to living with smaller animals. Always monitor their interactions and ensure that everyone feels secure and comfortable.

Bullmastiffs, with their natural calmness and easy-going nature, can bring a sense of stability and comfort to the lives of their fellow furry friends. They have an uncanny ability to read social cues and adjust their behavior accordingly, fostering an environment of trust and respect. Their presence often has a calming effect on other pets, creating a harmonious atmosphere within the household.

Remember, the key to a successful relationship between a Bullmastiff and other pets lies in proper introductions, gradual acclimatization, and ongoing positive reinforcement training. By creating a positive and nurturing environment, filled with love, patience, and understanding, you can build a bond between your Bullmastiff and other pets that will bring immeasurable joy and companionship to all involved.

So, open your heart and your home to the possibilities of a multi-pet household, and let the Bullmastiff's natural affinity for companionship and their gentle spirit enrich the lives of both you and your furry family members.

Bullmastiffs as Guard Dogs

When it comes to protecting their loved ones and their territory, Bullmastiffs shine as natural-born guardians. With their imposing presence and unwavering loyalty, they possess the innate qualities that make them excellent guard dogs. But what sets them apart from the rest is their unique approach to guarding, rooted in their calm and gentle nature.

Bullmastiffs have a natural instinct to protect their families and their homes. This instinct is deeply ingrained in their history as estate guardians, where they were bred to deter intruders and safeguard their surroundings. Their large size and powerful build serve as a visual deterrent, giving pause to those who might have ill intentions.

But what makes Bullmastiffs truly exceptional as guard dogs is their temperament. They are not aggressive or hyper-vigilant by nature. Instead, they possess a calm and even-tempered demeanor, which allows them to make rational decisions and respond appropriately to perceived threats. Their watchful and attentive nature helps them assess situations, ensuring that their protective response is proportionate to the perceived danger.

Bullmastiffs are known for their remarkable ability to distinguish between real threats and everyday situations. They are not inclined to be reactive or aggressive without cause. Their natural instinct is to assess the situation and respond accordingly. This makes them reliable guard dogs, as they are less likely to display unnecessary aggression or become a liability in a family setting.

Their protective nature extends not only to their human family members but also to their territory. Bullmastiffs are highly territorial dogs, fiercely defending their home and surroundings. They have a strong sense of ownership and will go to great lengths to protect what they perceive as their responsibility. This makes them excellent deterrents to potential intruders, as their presence alone can discourage any unwelcome visitors.

It's important to note that while Bullmastiffs have the potential to excel as guard dogs, their protective instincts need to be carefully managed and channeled through proper training and socialization. Early socialization allows them to differentiate between normal interactions and genuine threats, ensuring that their response is appropriate. Ongoing training, using positive reinforcement methods, helps to establish boundaries and reinforce their role as protectors without encouraging unnecessary aggression.

Another aspect that contributes to their effectiveness as guard dogs is their loyalty. Bullmastiffs form deep bonds with their families and consider their well-being as their utmost priority. They are dedicated and fiercely loyal, willing to put themselves in harm's way to protect their loved ones. This unwavering devotion makes them an invaluable asset in any security-conscious household.

It's worth mentioning that while Bullmastiffs possess the qualities of a guard dog, they are also gentle and affectionate family companions. They are not solely focused on their guarding duties but rather embrace the balance of being loving and protective at the same time. They understand the distinction between their guarding role and their role as a trusted family member, providing comfort, companionship, and unwavering love.

In conclusion, Bullmastiffs possess the ideal combination of temperament and protective instinct to excel as guard dogs. Their calm and even-tempered nature, combined with their loyalty and protective instincts, make them natural guardians of their families and homes. With the right training, socialization, and responsible ownership, Bullmastiffs can fulfill their role as protectors while remaining a beloved and cherished part of the family. So, rest easy knowing that your Bullmastiff is standing watch, ready to protect and love you with all their heart.

Training and Its Impact on Temperament

Training plays a pivotal role in shaping a Bullmastiff's temperament, transforming their inherent traits into well-rounded and obedient companions. The impact of training on their temperament cannot be overstated, as it shapes their behavior, enhances their social skills, and strengthens the bond between dog and owner.

Bullmastiffs are intelligent dogs with a strong desire to please their owners. This makes them highly receptive to training and eager learners. They thrive in an environment that provides structure, consistency, and positive reinforcement. Training not only helps them develop good manners and obedience but also instills confidence and a sense of purpose in their lives.

One of the primary goals of training a Bullmastiff is to establish clear boundaries and expectations. This begins with basic obedience training, teaching them essential commands such as sit, stay, come, and heel. By learning and obeying these commands, Bullmastiffs become more manageable and better able to navigate the world around them.

Positive reinforcement is a highly effective training method for Bullmastiffs. This approach involves rewarding desirable behaviors with treats, praise, or play, reinforcing the notion that good behavior is rewarded. Positive reinforcement creates a positive association and motivates Bullmastiffs to continue exhibiting appropriate behavior.

Training also helps Bullmastiffs develop social skills and appropriate behavior towards people and other animals. Early socialization is crucial, as it exposes them to a variety of people, animals, and environments, allowing them to become comfortable and well-adjusted in different situations. Through socialization, Bullmastiffs learn to interact politely, play gently, and be confident in various social settings. Consistency is key when training a Bullmastiff.

Establishing consistent routines, expectations, and consequences for their actions helps them understand boundaries and avoid confusion. Everyone in the household should be on the same page and follow the same training methods, ensuring that the Bullmastiff receives consistent guidance and reinforcement.

Training has a significant impact on a Bullmastiff's temperament by promoting good behavior and preventing potential issues. Through training, they learn self-control, patience, and appropriate responses to various stimuli. They become more adaptable and well-behaved, which enhances their overall temperament and makes them a pleasure to have as part of the family.

It's important to note that training should always be carried out in a positive and humane manner. Harsh or punitive training methods can be detrimental to a Bullmastiff's temperament and trust in their owners. Instead, focus on building a strong and positive bond through reward-based training, praise, and patience. Training is an ongoing process throughout a Bullmastiff's life. It doesn't stop after basic obedience is achieved. Continual training helps maintain good behavior, reinforces existing skills, and introduces new challenges. Advanced training, such as agility or therapy work, can provide mental stimulation and further enhance their temperament.

The impact of training on a Bullmastiff's temperament goes beyond the immediate benefits. It strengthens the bond between dog and owner, builds trust, and fosters a sense of mutual respect. A well-trained Bullmastiff is a confident, well-behaved, and balanced companion, ready to face any situation with grace and obedience.

So, invest time and effort in training your Bullmastiff, understanding that the impact goes far beyond basic obedience. Embrace the journey of training as an opportunity to shape their temperament, unlock their full potential, and deepen the connection between you and your beloved Bullmastiff. Together, you'll embark on an incredible adventure of learning, growth, and a lifelong partnership based on trust and understanding.

Common Misconceptions About Their Temperament

Ah, misconceptions – those sneaky ideas that can sometimes cloud our judgment and prevent us from truly understanding a breed. When it comes to Bullmastiffs, there are a few common misconceptions about their temperament that deserve to be debunked. So, let's shed some light on these misunderstandings and set the record straight!

Misconception #1: Bullmastiffs are aggressive. This couldn't be further from the truth! While Bullmastiffs are protective and have a strong instinct to guard, they are not inherently aggressive. Their calm and gentle nature shines through, making them loving and loyal companions. With proper socialization and training, Bullmastiffs can differentiate between genuine threats and everyday situations, responding appropriately and without unnecessary aggression.

Misconception #2: Bullmastiffs are mean-spirited or ill-tempered. Quite the contrary! Bullmastiffs are known for their even-tempered nature and stable temperament. They are often described as "gentle giants" due to their gentle and patient demeanor, particularly with children. Their loving and affectionate nature makes them wonderful family pets, and their calm presence brings comfort and joy to those around them.

Misconception #3: Bullmastiffs cannot be trusted with children or other pets. This couldn't be further from the truth! Bullmastiffs have a natural affinity for children and often form strong bonds with them. They are known to be patient and tolerant, understanding the delicate nature of little ones. With proper socialization and supervision, Bullmastiffs can coexist harmoniously with other pets as well. It's important to introduce them gradually and ensure that interactions are positive and controlled, setting the stage for a peaceful and loving relationship.

Misconception #4: Bullmastiffs require harsh or heavy-handed training methods. Nothing could be further from the truth! Bullmastiffs respond exceptionally well to positive reinforcement training methods. These methods focus on rewarding desirable behaviors, using treats, praise, and play as incentives. Harsh or heavy-handed training techniques can have a negative impact on their temperament and damage the bond of trust between dog and owner. By employing gentle and positive training methods, you can shape a Bullmastiff's temperament in a way that encourages their natural qualities and enhances their overall behavior.

Misconception #5: Bullmastiffs are overly dominant or stubborn. While every dog has its own unique personality, Bullmastiffs, in general, are not excessively dominant or stubborn. They have a natural inclination to please their owners and are eager learners. With consistent training, patience, and positive reinforcement, Bullmastiffs can become well-behaved and cooperative companions.

Misconception #6: Bullmastiffs require constant exercise and stimulation. While it's important to provide Bullmastiffs with regular exercise and mental stimulation, they are not a breed that requires excessive amounts of activity. Bullmastiffs have a moderate exercise requirement, enjoying leisurely walks and playtime in the yard. They are content to spend quality time with their families, soaking up love and companionship. However, it's important to strike a balance and ensure they receive appropriate exercise to maintain their overall health and well-being.
It's crucial to dispel these misconceptions and instead embrace the truth about Bullmastiffs' temperament.

They are gentle, loving, and loyal companions who bring immense joy and happiness to their families. By understanding their true nature and providing them with the love, training, and care they deserve, Bullmastiffs can thrive and become cherished members of any household.

So, let go of these misconceptions and open your heart to the truth about Bullmastiffs. Discover the incredible love, loyalty, and companionship they offer. Embrace their calm and gentle nature, and you'll experience a bond like no other – a bond built on trust, understanding, and the beauty of embracing a breed for who they truly are.

CHAPTER 4: BULLMASTIFFS AND HEALTH

In this chapter, we delve into the world of Bullmastiff health, exploring their typical health status, common health issues, lifespan, the importance of regular veterinary check-ups, the role of diet in their well-being, genetic health concerns, signs of a healthy Bullmastiff, and more. The health of our beloved companions is of utmost importance, so let's embark on this journey of understanding and caring for Bullmastiffs.

Bullmastiffs are generally considered a healthy breed, but like any living beings, they can be susceptible to certain health issues. Understanding these potential concerns and taking proactive measures can help ensure your Bullmastiff leads a happy and healthy life.

Regular veterinary check-ups are essential in maintaining your Bullmastiff's health. These check-ups allow your veterinarian to monitor their overall well-being, identify any potential health issues, and provide necessary preventive care. It's important to schedule routine vaccinations, dental cleanings, and screenings for common health conditions.

When it comes to nutrition, a well-balanced diet is key to a Bullmastiff's health and longevity. Feeding them high-quality, age-appropriate dog food that meets their nutritional needs is crucial. Consult with your veterinarian to determine the best diet for your Bullmastiff's specific age, activity level, and any specific health considerations.
Bullmastiffs have an average lifespan of 8 to 10 years.

However, with proper care, nutrition, exercise, and regular veterinary check-ups, they can live longer and healthier lives. Being proactive in their health care and providing them with a nurturing environment greatly contributes to their overall well-being.

While Bullmastiffs are generally healthy, there are some health conditions that are more commonly observed in the breed. These include hip and elbow dysplasia, which are conditions affecting the joints, and certain types of cancer, such as lymphoma and mast cell tumors. Regular veterinary examinations and screening tests can help identify these conditions early, allowing for timely intervention and treatment. Genetic health concerns are also prevalent in Bullmastiffs. Responsible breeders take steps to minimize the occurrence of these conditions by performing health screenings on breeding dogs and selecting breeding pairs that are free of known genetic issues. Some of the genetic health concerns in Bullmastiffs include heart conditions, eye disorders, and certain types of skin problems. Working with a reputable breeder who prioritizes health testing is crucial when adding a Bullmastiff to your family.

Signs of a healthy Bullmastiff include a shiny coat, clear and bright eyes, healthy weight and appetite, good muscle tone, and overall alertness and vitality. Regular exercise, mental stimulation, proper nutrition, and attention to their grooming needs contribute to their overall well-being and appearance.

In caring for your Bullmastiff's health, it's important to be aware of their specific needs and potential health concerns. Maintaining a close relationship with your veterinarian, following their recommendations for preventive care, and being attentive to any changes in your Bullmastiff's behavior or appearance are vital in providing the best possible care.

Remember, your Bullmastiff relies on you to be their advocate and caretaker. By prioritizing their health and well-being through regular check-ups, a nutritious diet, appropriate exercise, and a loving environment, you can ensure that your Bullmastiff enjoys a long and fulfilling life by your side.

So, let's embark on this journey of health together, arming ourselves with knowledge and taking the necessary steps to keep our Bullmastiffs in optimal health. They deserve nothing less than our utmost care and dedication to their well-being.

Typical Health Status of the Breed

When it comes to the health of Bullmastiffs, the good news is that they are generally a healthy breed. Like any living beings, they can experience health issues, but with proper care and attention, you can help ensure your Bullmastiff leads a happy and healthy life.

One of the reasons Bullmastiffs are known for their overall good health is the careful breeding practices that many responsible breeders adhere to. These breeders prioritize the health and well-being of their dogs, conducting health screenings and selecting breeding pairs with the aim of minimizing the occurrence of genetic health issues in their offspring.

In terms of physical health, Bullmastiffs are known for their robust build and sturdy frame. They have a strong and muscular body, which contributes to their overall strength and resilience. This physical strength, coupled with their balanced proportions, allows them to move with grace and agility despite their size.

In addition to their physical health, Bullmastiffs have a generally sound temperament and stable emotional well-being. They are known for their calm and gentle nature, which contributes to their overall mental health and emotional stability. This temperament, combined with their loyalty and devotion, makes them excellent family companions and loving protectors.

While Bullmastiffs are considered a healthy breed, it's important to remember that they can still be susceptible to certain health conditions. Like many large and giant breeds, they may be prone to developing joint issues, such as hip and elbow dysplasia. These conditions involve abnormal development of the joints, leading to discomfort and potential mobility issues. Regular veterinary check-ups, proper nutrition, and appropriate exercise can help minimize the impact of these conditions.

Another health concern that can affect Bullmastiffs is certain types of cancer. Lymphoma and mast cell tumors are more commonly observed in the breed. Early detection through regular veterinary examinations and proactive screening can aid in the timely treatment and management of these conditions, potentially improving outcomes.

To ensure the ongoing health and well-being of your Bullmastiff, it's essential to establish a strong relationship with a trusted veterinarian. Regular check-ups, vaccinations, and preventive care are crucial in maintaining their health. Your veterinarian can provide guidance on vaccinations, flea and tick prevention, heartworm prevention, and other aspects of preventive healthcare specific to your Bullmastiff's needs.

Additionally, proper nutrition plays a vital role in keeping your Bullmastiff healthy. A balanced diet that meets their nutritional requirements, taking into account their age, activity level, and any specific health considerations, is key. Your veterinarian can help you determine the best diet for your Bullmastiff and provide guidance on feeding schedules and portion sizes.

Remember, while Bullmastiffs are generally healthy, each dog is an individual, and their health can vary. Paying attention to any changes in their behavior, appetite, or physical appearance is essential. If you notice anything unusual or concerning, it's always best to consult with your veterinarian for a thorough examination and appropriate guidance.

By staying proactive, providing proper care, and being attentive to their health needs, you can help your Bullmastiff enjoy a long and fulfilling life. Their health and happiness are in your hands, and with your love and commitment, you can ensure they thrive as the incredible companions they are meant to be.

Common Health Issues

While Bullmastiffs are generally a healthy breed, like any dog, they can be prone to certain health issues. Understanding these common health concerns can help you recognize and address potential problems early on, ensuring your Bullmastiff receives the necessary care and attention.

One of the common health issues seen in Bullmastiffs is hip dysplasia. This condition occurs when the hip joint doesn't develop properly, leading to discomfort and potentially affecting mobility. It's important to be mindful of the signs, such as difficulty rising or reluctance to engage in physical activity, and to consult with your veterinarian if you suspect hip dysplasia. X-rays and other diagnostic tests can help confirm the diagnosis, and your veterinarian may recommend treatment options such as medication, weight management, or even surgery in severe cases.

Another condition to be aware of is elbow dysplasia, which involves abnormal development of the elbow joint. This can cause pain, lameness, and joint dysfunction. Regular veterinary check-ups and monitoring your Bullmastiff's gait and movement can help detect any signs of elbow dysplasia. Treatment options may include medication, physical therapy, or in some cases, surgery.

Heart conditions can also be a concern for Bullmastiffs. Dilated cardiomyopathy (DCM) is a condition that affects the heart's ability to pump blood effectively. It's important to monitor your Bullmastiff for signs of heart disease, such as coughing, difficulty breathing, or weakness. Regular veterinary examinations, including heart screenings and echocardiograms, can aid in early detection and management of heart conditions.

Skin problems can occur in Bullmastiffs as well. They may be prone to allergies, which can manifest as itching, redness, or skin infections. Allergies can be triggered by various factors, including food, environmental allergens, or flea bites. Working closely with your veterinarian to identify and manage any allergies can help keep your Bullmastiff's skin healthy and comfortable.

Cancer is another health concern that can affect Bullmastiffs. They may be predisposed to certain types of cancer, including lymphoma and mast cell tumors. Regular veterinary check-ups, including thorough physical examinations and screening tests, can help detect any early signs of cancer. Treatment options may include surgery, chemotherapy, or other specialized treatments depending on the type and stage of cancer.

Eye issues can also be seen in Bullmastiffs. Entropion, a condition in which the eyelids roll inward, and ectropion, where the eyelids sag or roll outward, are common eyelid abnormalities. These conditions can cause discomfort and potentially lead to eye infections or corneal ulcers. Regular eye examinations and consultations with a veterinary ophthalmologist can help manage these conditions, with treatment options ranging from topical medications to surgical correction.

It's important to note that not all Bullmastiffs will develop these health issues, and with proper care, many can live long and healthy lives. Regular veterinary check-ups, preventive care, a nutritious diet, exercise, and a loving environment can contribute to their overall well-being and minimize the impact of potential health concerns.

Remember, if you notice any changes in your Bullmastiff's behavior, appetite, energy levels, or physical appearance, it's essential to consult with your veterinarian. Early detection and intervention can make a significant difference in managing health issues and maintaining your Bullmastiff's quality of life.

By being knowledgeable about common health concerns and partnering with your veterinarian, you can provide the best possible care for your Bullmastiff. Your commitment and proactive approach to their health will help ensure they lead a happy, healthy, and fulfilling life by your side.

Expected Lifespan

When welcoming a Bullmastiff into your life, it's natural to wonder about their expected lifespan. While individual factors and proper care play a role, Bullmastiffs typically have an average lifespan of 8 to 10 years. However, with exceptional care and attention to their health, it's possible for some Bullmastiffs to exceed this range.

Genetics, environment, nutrition, exercise, and preventive healthcare are all important factors that can influence a Bullmastiff's lifespan. Responsible breeders prioritize the health and longevity of their dogs by conducting health screenings and selecting breeding pairs with the aim of minimizing the occurrence of genetic health issues. By choosing a Bullmastiff from a reputable breeder who focuses on health, you increase the chances of your companion living a longer and healthier life.

Creating a nurturing environment and providing appropriate care are key in extending your Bullmastiff's lifespan. Regular veterinary check-ups, vaccinations, and preventive care are essential to maintaining their well-being. Your veterinarian will guide you on necessary vaccinations, flea and tick prevention, heartworm prevention, and other preventive measures tailored to your Bullmastiff's specific needs.

Nutrition plays a vital role in a Bullmastiff's overall health and lifespan. Feeding them a balanced diet, formulated for their age, size, and specific dietary requirements, is essential. Your veterinarian can provide guidance on appropriate food choices, portion sizes, and feeding schedules. Maintaining a healthy weight is important, as excess weight can contribute to joint problems and other health issues.

Exercise is another critical aspect of promoting longevity in Bullmastiffs. While they may not require intense exercise like some breeds, regular physical activity is necessary to keep them fit and mentally stimulated. Daily walks, interactive play sessions, and moderate exercise help keep their muscles toned, maintain a healthy weight, and prevent boredom. Be mindful not to overexert them, especially in hot weather, as they can be prone to heat exhaustion.

Additionally, providing mental stimulation is important for their overall well-being. Bullmastiffs are intelligent dogs and enjoy activities that challenge their minds. Puzzle toys, interactive games, and obedience training sessions can provide mental enrichment, keeping their minds sharp and engaged. It's worth mentioning that while Bullmastiffs have an average lifespan of 8 to 10 years, individual variations occur.
Some Bullmastiffs may surpass this range, while others may have shorter lifespans due to various factors. Being attentive to their health, addressing any health concerns promptly, and maintaining a close relationship with your veterinarian can help maximize their quality of life.

Ultimately, the love, care, and attention you provide throughout their lives will significantly impact your Bullmastiff's longevity. By being proactive, prioritizing their well-being, and cherishing the precious moments together, you can make their years full of joy, happiness, and love. The bond you share will endure for a lifetime, and the memories you create will remain in your heart forever.

The Role of Regular Veterinary Check-ups

Regular veterinary check-ups play a crucial role in maintaining the health and well-being of your beloved Bullmastiff. These check-ups are not just a routine formality but an essential part of responsible pet ownership. By ensuring that your Bullmastiff receives regular veterinary care, you can address potential health concerns early on, provide preventive care, and promote their overall longevity.

During a veterinary check-up, your veterinarian will perform a comprehensive examination of your Bullmastiff. They will assess various aspects of their health, including their weight, body condition, coat, eyes, ears, teeth, heart, lungs, and overall physical condition. This examination allows the veterinarian to detect any abnormalities, monitor changes, and identify potential health issues that may require further investigation or treatment.
One of the primary benefits of regular check-ups is the opportunity for preventive care. Your veterinarian will discuss and administer vaccinations to protect your Bullmastiff against common infectious diseases.

Vaccinations are crucial in preventing potentially life-threatening illnesses, such as parvovirus, distemper, and rabies. Your veterinarian will create a vaccination schedule tailored to your Bullmastiff's needs and ensure they receive the necessary boosters throughout their lives.

In addition to vaccinations, regular check-ups allow for the administration of preventive treatments. Your veterinarian may recommend and provide flea and tick preventives, heartworm prevention medications, and deworming treatments. These preventive measures safeguard your Bullmastiff from parasites and the potential health risks associated with infestations.

Beyond vaccinations and preventive treatments, regular veterinary check-ups also provide an opportunity to discuss your Bullmastiff's diet, nutrition, and overall lifestyle. Your veterinarian can provide guidance on selecting an appropriate diet, portion sizes, and feeding schedules to meet your Bullmastiff's specific needs. They can address any concerns you may have regarding weight management, dietary supplements, or special dietary requirements.

Furthermore, regular check-ups allow your veterinarian to monitor your Bullmastiff's growth and development. This is especially important during their early months and years when they are rapidly growing and maturing. Your veterinarian can assess their growth rate, bone development, and ensure they are reaching their milestones appropriately. Early identification of any developmental concerns or growth abnormalities can help prevent long-term issues and provide necessary interventions if required.

Regular veterinary check-ups are also an excellent opportunity for you to discuss any behavioral concerns or changes you may have noticed in your Bullmastiff. Your veterinarian can provide guidance on training, behavior modification, or refer you to a professional dog trainer or behaviorist if needed.

Addressing behavioral issues early can help foster a harmonious relationship between you and your Bullmastiff while ensuring their mental well-being. Ultimately, regular veterinary check-ups are about proactive healthcare and preventive medicine. They are a chance to catch potential health issues in their early stages, allowing for prompt intervention and treatment. By attending these check-ups, you demonstrate your commitment to your Bullmastiff's well-being and provide them with the best possible care.

Remember, your veterinarian is your trusted partner in your Bullmastiff's health journey. Building a strong and open relationship with them allows for effective communication, personalized care, and the shared goal of promoting your Bullmastiff's longevity and quality of life.

So, mark those check-up dates on your calendar, and embrace the opportunity to work together with your veterinarian in safeguarding the health and happiness of your beloved Bullmastiff. With regular check-ups, preventive care, and your unwavering dedication, you can provide them with a lifetime of love, care, and good health.

The Importance of Diet in Health

When it comes to the health of your Bullmastiff, diet plays a crucial role. Providing them with a nutritious and well-balanced diet is essential for their overall well-being, energy levels, immune system, and longevity. Let's explore the importance of diet and how it contributes to the health of your beloved Bullmastiff.

A healthy diet is the foundation of good health for any dog, including Bullmastiffs. It provides them with the essential nutrients, vitamins, and minerals necessary for growth, development, and maintaining optimal body function. A diet tailored to their specific needs ensures they receive the right balance of proteins, carbohydrates, fats, and other essential nutrients.

Bullmastiffs have specific dietary requirements based on their age, size, activity level, and any specific health considerations. Puppies require a diet that supports their rapid growth and development, while adult Bullmastiffs need a diet that sustains their energy levels and maintains their ideal body condition. Senior Bullmastiffs may have different dietary needs, such as joint support or lower-calorie options to manage weight.

Consulting with your veterinarian is key to determining the appropriate diet for your Bullmastiff.

They can evaluate your dog's individual needs and recommend a high-quality commercial dog food or provide guidance on preparing a balanced homemade diet. It's important to choose a reputable brand that uses quality ingredients and meets the nutritional standards set by regulatory bodies.

The quality and composition of the diet directly impact your Bullmastiff's health. A diet rich in high-quality proteins, such as meat, fish, or poultry, helps support their muscle development and overall strength. Complex carbohydrates from sources like whole grains and vegetables provide sustained energy and dietary fiber for proper digestion.

The right balance of fats is also crucial. Essential fatty acids, such as omega-3 and omega-6, support a healthy coat, skin, and immune system. Incorporating these healthy fats from sources like fish oil, flaxseed, or poultry fat can promote a glossy coat and reduce inflammation.

It's important to feed your Bullmastiff the appropriate portion sizes to maintain a healthy weight. Obesity can lead to various health issues, such as joint problems, heart strain, and decreased mobility. Your veterinarian can provide guidance on portion sizes and feeding schedules, taking into consideration your Bullmastiff's age, weight, and activity level.

Remember to provide fresh and clean water at all times. Hydration is vital for your Bullmastiff's overall health, digestion, and proper bodily functions. Ensure that their water bowl is readily accessible and refilled regularly.

While a balanced diet is essential, it's equally important to avoid feeding your Bullmastiff harmful foods. Certain human foods, such as chocolate, grapes, onions, and caffeine, can be toxic to dogs. Additionally, avoid feeding them excessive amounts of table scraps or fatty foods, as these can lead to digestive upsets and weight gain.

Monitoring your Bullmastiff's body condition is crucial. Regularly assess their weight, body shape, and overall appearance. Your veterinarian can guide you on maintaining an ideal body condition score, which helps ensure that your Bullmastiff is neither underweight nor overweight.

In addition to a nutritious diet, treats can be used as rewards and for training purposes. Opt for healthy, dog-specific treats that are low in calories and free from artificial additives. Treats should only constitute a small portion of their overall daily caloric intake.

By providing your Bullmastiff with a well-balanced diet, tailored to their specific needs, you are setting the stage for their overall health, vitality, and longevity. A healthy diet, combined with regular exercise, mental stimulation, and veterinary care, ensures your Bullmastiff thrives as a happy and healthy companion.

So, let's embrace the importance of diet in maintaining the health of our Bullmastiffs. With your commitment to providing a nutritious and balanced diet, you are paving the way for a lifetime of good health, boundless energy, and endless joy together.

Genetic Health Concerns

Genetic health concerns are an important aspect to consider when it comes to Bullmastiffs. While they are generally a healthy breed, like many purebred dogs, they can be prone to certain genetic health conditions. Understanding these concerns and working with responsible breeders can help mitigate the risks and ensure the overall health of your Bullmastiff.

Responsible breeders are committed to breeding healthy Bullmastiffs and take proactive measures to minimize the occurrence of genetic health issues in their breeding lines. They perform health screenings on their breeding dogs, such as hip and elbow evaluations, cardiac exams, and eye examinations.

These screenings aim to identify potential genetic issues and select breeding pairs that are less likely to pass on these conditions to their offspring.
One common genetic health concern in Bullmastiffs is hip and elbow dysplasia. This condition involves the abnormal development of the hip and elbow joints, leading to discomfort, lameness, and potential arthritis. Regular screening tests, such as hip and elbow evaluations conducted by certified organizations, can help identify dogs with good joint health for breeding purposes. Working with a reputable breeder who prioritizes these screenings greatly reduces the risk of your Bullmastiff developing hip or elbow dysplasia.

Heart conditions, including cardiomyopathy, can also be of concern in Bullmastiffs. Cardiomyopathy is a disease that affects the heart muscle, impairing its ability to pump blood effectively. Regular cardiac evaluations, such as echocardiograms and auscultations, can help detect any signs of heart disease early on, allowing for appropriate management and treatment.

Eye disorders are another genetic health concern in Bullmastiffs. Conditions such as entropion, ectropion, and progressive retinal atrophy (PRA) can affect their vision and overall ocular health. Regular eye examinations performed by a veterinary ophthalmologist can help identify these conditions and provide guidance on appropriate treatment or management options.

Certain types of skin problems can also be genetically linked in Bullmastiffs. These can include allergies, dermatitis, and various skin infections. While not all skin issues are strictly genetic, predisposition to certain conditions may be hereditary. Working closely with your veterinarian and maintaining proper skincare practices, such as regular grooming, can help minimize the impact of these skin concerns.

It's important to note that responsible breeders prioritize the health and well-being of their dogs and aim to minimize the occurrence of genetic health issues. By obtaining a Bullmastiff from a reputable breeder who conducts health screenings and provides proper care for their breeding dogs, you greatly increase the likelihood of your Bullmastiff being free from these genetic health concerns.

While genetic health concerns exist, it's essential to remember that not all Bullmastiffs will develop these conditions. Responsible breeding practices, regular veterinary check-ups, proper nutrition, and a loving environment contribute to their overall health and well-being. By partnering with a reputable breeder and being proactive in their care, you are taking significant steps to minimize the risk and provide your Bullmastiff with the best possible start in life.

Remember, your Bullmastiff's genetic health is just one aspect of their overall well-being. The love, care, and attention you provide throughout their life journey will make a tremendous difference in their happiness and longevity. With responsible breeding practices and your unwavering commitment, you can ensure your Bullmastiff thrives as a healthy and cherished member of your family.

POINT 7: SIGNS OF A HEALTHY BULLMASTIFF

When it comes to the well-being of your Bullmastiff, being able to recognize the signs of a healthy dog is crucial. By observing and understanding these indicators, you can ensure that your Bullmastiff is in optimal health and take prompt action if any concerns arise. Here are some key signs to look out for that indicate a healthy Bullmastiff:

1. **Energy and Vitality:** A healthy Bullmastiff will exhibit a good level of energy and vitality. They will be alert, responsive, and eager to participate in activities. Whether it's going for walks, playing fetch, or simply enjoying quality time with you, they will demonstrate enthusiasm and an overall zest for life.

2. **Appetite and Weight Management:** A healthy Bullmastiff will have a healthy appetite and maintain an appropriate weight for their age, size, and breed. They should display a consistent interest in their food and maintain a stable weight without being excessively underweight or overweight. Regular feeding schedules and portion control can help ensure their nutritional needs are met.

3. **Smooth and Shiny Coat:** One of the telltale signs of a healthy Bullmastiff is a smooth and shiny coat. Their fur should be lustrous, free from excessive shedding, and without any bald patches or signs of irritation. Regular grooming, including brushing and bathing, can help maintain a healthy coat and minimize any skin issues.

4. **Healthy Skin:** In addition to a shiny coat, a healthy Bullmastiff will have clean and healthy skin. Their skin should be free from redness, rashes, or excessive dryness. It should feel supple and without any signs of inflammation or discomfort. Regular inspection and care, including keeping their skin clean and dry, can contribute to maintaining healthy skin.

5. **Clear Eyes and Ears:** Healthy Bullmastiffs have clear and bright eyes. Their eyes should be free from discharge, redness, or any signs of inflammation. Ears should also be clean, without excessive wax buildup or a foul odor. Regular cleaning and inspections can help

prevent ear infections and ensure their eyes and ears remain in good health.

6. **Fresh Breath and Dental Health:** Dental hygiene is important for your Bullmastiff's overall health. A healthy dog will have fresh breath and clean teeth. Regular dental care, including toothbrushing and professional cleanings as recommended by your veterinarian, can help maintain their oral health and prevent dental diseases.

7. **Good Digestive Function:** A healthy Bullmastiff will have regular and well-formed bowel movements. Their stools should be of normal consistency and color, indicating good digestive function. Any sudden changes in bowel habits, such as diarrhea or constipation, should be promptly addressed with veterinary attention.

8. **Positive Mental Well-being:** A healthy Bullmastiff will exhibit positive mental well-being. They should be emotionally stable, displaying a balanced temperament and a happy demeanor. They will seek companionship, enjoy social interactions, and show trust and affection towards their family members.

9.
Remember, it's important to establish a strong partnership with your veterinarian and schedule regular wellness check-ups. These check-ups provide an opportunity for comprehensive examinations, vaccinations, and screenings to ensure your Bullmastiff's ongoing health. By being proactive and

attentive to their well-being, you can help your Bullmastiff lead a healthy and fulfilling life.

By closely monitoring these signs of a healthy Bullmastiff, you can gain valuable insights into their overall well-being. Promptly addressing any changes or concerns with your veterinarian ensures that your Bullmastiff receives the care they need and deserve. Your dedication to their health and happiness will contribute to a long and joyful journey together.

CHAPTER 5: NUTRITION NEEDS

In this chapter, we will explore the nutrition needs of your Bullmastiff. Proper nutrition is essential for their overall health, energy levels, and well-being. We will discuss the importance of a balanced diet, suitable food types, the role of hydration, and the significance of treats and supplements in their nutrition. Let's dive into the world of Bullmastiff nutrition and learn how to provide the best nourishment for your beloved companion.

As a responsible Bullmastiff owner, it's crucial to understand the specific nutritional requirements of your furry friend at different life stages. Each stage, from puppyhood to adulthood and into their senior years, comes with its own unique needs. By providing the right nutrients and a balanced diet, you can support their growth, development, and overall vitality.

During the puppy stage, your Bullmastiff experiences rapid growth and development. Their nutritional needs are different from adult dogs, and it's important to feed them accordingly. Look for high-quality puppy food specifically formulated for large breeds. These formulas contain the right balance of proteins, carbohydrates, vitamins, and minerals to support their growing bodies. Following the feeding guidelines on the packaging and adjusting portions as your puppy grows will ensure they receive the necessary nutrients for healthy development.

As your Bullmastiff transitions into adulthood, their nutritional needs change. A well-rounded diet that maintains their energy levels, supports their overall health, and helps them maintain an ideal weight is essential. Look for adult dog food designed specifically for large breeds. These formulas provide the necessary proteins, carbohydrates, fats, and essential nutrients to keep your Bullmastiff in optimal condition. Consider their activity level, weight, and any specific dietary requirements when determining the appropriate portion sizes.

When your Bullmastiff enters their senior years, their metabolism may slow down, and they may have specific health considerations. Senior-specific dog food can provide the nutritional support they need, such as joint health support, easy-to-digest ingredients, and antioxidants to support their aging immune system. Consult with your veterinarian to determine the right diet for your senior Bullmastiff and address any specific health concerns they may have.

Choosing the right food type for your Bullmastiff is essential. Opt for high-quality commercial dog food that prioritizes wholesome ingredients and avoids artificial additives or fillers. Look for products that list a quality source of animal protein, such as chicken, beef, or fish, as the main ingredient. Whole grains like brown rice or oatmeal can provide healthy carbohydrates, while fruits and vegetables offer important vitamins and minerals.

If you prefer to prepare homemade meals for your Bullmastiff, consult with a veterinary nutritionist to ensure they meet the necessary nutritional requirements. Homemade diets require careful planning to provide a well-balanced mix of proteins, carbohydrates, fats, and essential nutrients.

Proper hydration is another critical aspect of your Bullmastiff's nutrition. Fresh and clean water should always be available to them. Adequate hydration is important for digestion, temperature regulation, and overall bodily functions. Ensure that your Bullmastiff has access to water at all times, especially during hot weather or after physical activity.

Treats can be incorporated into your Bullmastiff's diet as rewards or for training purposes. However, it's important to choose treats that are appropriate for their size and nutritional needs. Opt for treats that are low in fat and made from wholesome ingredients. Avoid excessive treats, as they can contribute to weight gain and nutritional imbalances.

Supplements can be beneficial for your Bullmastiff's overall health, but it's important to consult with your veterinarian before adding any supplements to their diet. Your veterinarian can assess your Bullmastiff's specific needs and recommend appropriate supplements, such as joint supplements or omega-3 fatty acids for their coat and skin health.

Remember, nutrition plays a vital role in keeping your Bullmastiff healthy and happy. By providing a balanced diet, appropriate portion sizes, and ample hydration, you are setting the foundation for their well-being. Regularly assess their weight, body condition, and overall health, and consult with your veterinarian if you have any concerns or questions regarding their nutrition.

Puppy, Adult, and Senior Nutritional Needs

Understanding the nutritional needs of your Bullmastiff at different life stages is crucial for their growth, development, and overall well-being. By providing the right nutrition during their puppy, adult, and senior years, you can support their health and ensure they have the best quality of life. Let's explore the specific nutritional needs of Bullmastiffs at each stage.

Puppy Nutrition:
During the puppy stage, your Bullmastiff is undergoing rapid growth and development. Their nutritional requirements differ from those of adult dogs. Puppies need a diet that supports their energy needs, bone growth, and muscle development. Look for high-quality puppy food that is specifically formulated for large breed puppies. These formulas provide the right balance of nutrients, including

proteins, fats, vitamins, and minerals, to promote healthy growth. Feeding your Bullmastiff puppy food formulated for their specific needs will give them the best start in life.

Adult Nutrition:
Once your Bullmastiff reaches adulthood, their nutritional needs change. Adult Bullmastiffs require a balanced diet that supports their energy levels, maintains muscle mass, and keeps them in optimal condition. Look for adult dog food designed for large breed dogs. These formulas contain the necessary proteins, carbohydrates, fats, vitamins, and minerals to meet their nutritional needs. It's important to consider your Bullmastiff's activity level, weight, and overall health when determining the appropriate portion sizes. Regular exercise and a well-rounded diet will help them maintain their weight and overall health.

Senior Nutrition:
As your Bullmastiff enters their senior years, their metabolism may slow down, and they may have specific health concerns. Senior Bullmastiffs may benefit from a diet that supports joint health, digestive health, and overall vitality. Look for senior-specific dog food that is formulated to meet the nutritional needs of aging dogs. These formulas often include ingredients such as glucosamine and chondroitin to support joint health, easily digestible proteins, and antioxidants to support their immune system. It's essential to consult with your veterinarian to determine the best diet for your senior Bullmastiff and address any specific health concerns they may have.

Regardless of their life stage, it's important to provide your Bullmastiff with a balanced and nutritious diet. This includes high-quality protein sources, such as meat or fish, to support their muscle development and maintenance. Carbohydrates, such as whole grains or vegetables, provide energy. Fats, in moderation, contribute to a healthy coat and skin. Additionally, make sure your Bullmastiff has access to fresh and clean water at all times to stay hydrated.

Remember, the nutritional needs of your Bullmastiff may vary depending on factors such as their age, activity level, and overall health. Regular monitoring of their weight, body condition, and overall well-being is essential. If you have any concerns or questions about their nutritional needs, consult with your veterinarian for personalized guidance. Providing the right nutrition tailored to each life stage will help ensure a happy, healthy life for your Bullmastiff.

Suggested Food Types

Choosing the right food for your Bullmastiff is crucial for their overall health and well-being. Providing a well-balanced diet that meets their nutritional needs is essential at every stage of their life. Here, we will explore suggested food types that can contribute to a healthy and nutritious diet for your Bullmastiff.

1. **High-Quality Commercial Dog Food:** Opting for high-quality commercial dog food formulated for large breeds is a convenient and reliable choice. Look for brands that prioritize

wholesome ingredients and avoid artificial additives or fillers. Check the product label for a quality source of animal protein, such as chicken, beef, or fish, listed as the main ingredient. These proteins are essential for muscle development and maintenance. Additionally, whole grains like brown rice or oatmeal can provide healthy carbohydrates, while fruits and vegetables offer important vitamins and minerals.

2. **Raw or Fresh Food Diet:** Some Bullmastiff owners choose to feed their dogs a raw or fresh food diet. This approach involves feeding uncooked meats, bones, fruits, vegetables, and sometimes organ meats. If you decide to go this route, it's crucial to consult with a veterinary nutritionist or your veterinarian to ensure that the diet meets your Bullmastiff's specific nutritional needs. They can guide you in selecting the right balance of ingredients and provide advice on food preparation and safety.

3. **Homemade Diets:** If you prefer to prepare homemade meals for your Bullmastiff, it's important to seek guidance from a veterinary nutritionist. Homemade diets require careful planning to ensure they provide the necessary balance of proteins, carbohydrates, fats, vitamins, and minerals. Consulting with a professional will help ensure that your homemade meals meet your Bullmastiff's specific nutritional requirements and avoid any deficiencies.

4. **Prescription Diets:** In some cases, your Bullmastiff may have specific dietary needs due to health conditions. In such situations, your veterinarian may recommend prescription diets that address these specific concerns. These diets are designed to manage conditions such as allergies, digestive issues, or joint problems. If your Bullmastiff requires a prescription diet, follow your veterinarian's recommendations closely to ensure they receive the appropriate nutrition.

It's important to note that whatever diet you choose for your Bullmastiff, it's essential to provide a balanced and complete nutrition. Avoid feeding them foods that are toxic to dogs, such as chocolate, onions, garlic, grapes, and raisins. These can be harmful and should be strictly avoided.

When transitioning your Bullmastiff to a new diet, it's recommended to do so gradually over a period of several days. Start by mixing small amounts of the new food with their current food, gradually increasing the proportion of the new food. This gradual transition helps prevent digestive upset and allows your Bullmastiff's system to adjust to the new diet. Remember to monitor your Bullmastiff's weight, body condition, and overall health regularly. Adjust their portion sizes accordingly to maintain an optimal weight. It's also important to provide them with access to fresh and clean water at all times to ensure proper hydration.

By selecting appropriate food types and following a balanced and nutritious diet, you can provide your

Bullmastiff with the essential nutrients they need to thrive. If you have any concerns or questions about their diet, consult with your veterinarian for personalized advice and guidance.

Foods to Avoid

As we've journeyed together into the world of Bullmastiffs, we've discovered many of their needs and quirks. Now, it's time to dish out some crucial "no-no's" when it comes to our gentle giants' dietary needs. Just as there are power-packed foods that can bolster our Bullmastiffs' health, there are also certain foods that, while they might seem harmless, can actually be harmful to our pets.

Let's envision you're cooking up a feast in your kitchen. The savory smell fills the house and catches the attention of your four-legged buddy. Those beautiful, expressive Bullmastiff eyes are staring at you, silently pleading for a tidbit. It's hard to resist, isn't it? But wait, before you give in, it's essential to know which foods from your plate are safe for your Bullmastiff to consume, and which ones should be strictly off-limits.

Among the prime offenders in the "foods to avoid" list are chocolate, onions, and garlic. These are toxic to most dogs, and the Bullmastiff is no exception. Chocolate contains theobromine, a compound dogs cannot process efficiently, leading to potential poisoning. Onions and garlic, on the other hand, can lead to anemia by damaging the red blood cells. Remember, it's not just whole onions or garlic cloves we're talking about, but any food that's been seasoned with these ingredients as well.

Alcohol and caffeine are big no-no's too. While it might seem obvious, it's worth emphasizing. These substances can cause serious health issues, including nervous system problems and rapid heart rate. The same goes for the artificial sweetener xylitol, often found in sugar-free gums, candies, and even some types of peanut butter. It can induce a rapid and dangerous drop in a dog's blood sugar levels and potentially lead to liver failure.

Fatty and rich foods are also troublesome. Your Bullmastiff may drool as you munch on that greasy slice of bacon, but these high-fat foods can lead to conditions like pancreatitis. Over time, consistent exposure to such foods can contribute to obesity and other health issues.

And remember those pits and seeds from fruits like peaches, plums, and cherries? They can be choking hazards and, when ingested, can lead to serious intestinal blockages. Plus, the pits from these fruits contain a chemical that can break down into cyanide in the body.

Finally, raw yeast dough is something to be cautious of. If your Bullmastiff accidentally ingests some, the dough could expand in their stomach, causing significant discomfort and potentially serious complications.

Navigating the do's and don'ts of your Bullmastiff's diet can seem daunting, but remember, every time you help your pet avoid these problematic foods, you're taking a step towards ensuring their long, healthy, and happy life by your side.

Role of Nutrition in Weight Management

As a Bullmastiff owner, you're no stranger to the grand size of these gentle giants. Weighing anywhere between 100 to 130 pounds, these dogs have a commanding presence that's simply hard to ignore. But with this large size comes a big responsibility - weight management.

Imagine you're packing for a long trek up a mountain. Every item you add to your backpack matters, right? Too light, and you might not have all the necessary supplies, but too heavy, and the journey becomes unnecessarily hard. This is very similar to how nutrition plays a vital role in managing your Bullmastiff's weight.

Just like us humans, dogs need a balanced diet to maintain a healthy weight. This balance is a juggling act between the energy (calories) that goes into their bodies and the energy they expend during the day. If the balance tips with too much intake and not enough exercise, our Bullmastiffs can end up carrying excess weight.

Obesity in Bullmastiffs is a real concern, as it can lead to a plethora of health problems, from heart disease to diabetes and even joint issues, particularly given their large size. It's like our hypothetical backpack becoming too heavy, making the climb up the mountain that much more strenuous.

So, what's the role of nutrition in this balancing act? Well, it's all about quality, quantity, and timing. The quality of food plays a pivotal role because not all calories are created equal. For example, the calories derived from a lean chicken breast are far more nutritious than those from a piece of bacon. Bullmastiffs need a diet rich in high-quality proteins, balanced with healthy fats, and a moderate amount of complex carbohydrates.

Next comes quantity. Even the highest quality food can contribute to weight gain if served in large portions. It's important to feed your Bullmastiff an appropriate amount for their size, age, and activity level. Speaking of activity, remember, the energy equation isn't just about food. Regular exercise is vital to help burn off those calories and keep your Bullmastiff in good shape.

Finally, let's talk about timing. Regular feeding schedules and portion control can do wonders in managing your Bullmastiff's weight. Random, free-feeding habits can lead to overeating, while routine meal times can create a rhythm that complements their metabolism and energy levels.

In the grand trek of life, managing your Bullmastiff's weight through proper nutrition is like packing the perfect backpack - it's not about stuffing it full or leaving it empty but finding the right balance. This way, you and your Bullmastiff companion can enjoy the journey, every step of the way, as healthy and happy as can be.

Effect of Nutrition on Skin and Coat Health

Imagine the first time you met a Bullmastiff. You were probably struck by their imposing size, but also their beautiful, thick coat and soft skin underneath. There's something almost hypnotic about running your fingers through their smooth, dense fur. Just like their big heart and their robust stature, a Bullmastiff's coat is an essential part of their charm. And just like their heart and body, it requires special care, a significant part of which comes from their nutrition.

Think about how you feel when you've been eating a well-balanced, nutritious diet. You're not just healthier on the inside, right? Your skin has a particular glow to it, and your hair shines a bit brighter. The same principle applies to our Bullmastiff buddies. Their skin and coat health is a direct reflection of what they consume.

A Bullmastiff's coat isn't just for looks or petting, though. It's their first line of defense against the outside world, protecting them from elements like sun, cold, and various allergens. Just beneath, their skin is an integral part of their immune system. So, keeping both in top shape is crucial, and that's where nutrition steps into the spotlight.

A well-balanced diet plays a vital role in maintaining your Bullmastiff's glossy coat and healthy skin. High-quality proteins, for instance, provide the building blocks for skin and hair cells. Without enough protein, you might notice that your Bullmastiff's coat looks dull or brittle.

Then, we have fats, particularly Omega-3 and Omega-6 fatty acids. These are like the magic elixir for your Bullmastiff's coat, giving it that beautiful shine we all adore. They also aid in keeping the skin underneath hydrated and supple, preventing issues like dryness and flaking.

Let's not forget about vitamins and minerals, the unsung heroes of nutrition. For instance, vitamin E helps protect the skin cells from oxidative damage, while zinc plays a vital role in skin health and wound healing. Biotin, a B-vitamin, is another key player, often dubbed the 'hair vitamin,' contributing to a thick, glossy coat.

As you see, feeding your Bullmastiff isn't just about keeping them full or even just about managing their weight. It's about providing them with a balanced diet that nourishes them from the inside out, keeping their skin healthy and their coat glowing. So next time you're watching your Bullmastiff romping around, their coat gleaming in the sun, remember that each strand of that glossy fur is a testament to the balanced nutrition you're providing them with.
A healthy Bullmastiff is a happy Bullmastiff, and a happy Bullmastiff makes for a delighted owner.

Overall Importance of a Balanced Diet

As we continue our journey with our Bullmastiffs, it becomes increasingly clear that caring for these gentle giants involves more than just love and attention. It's also about providing them with the right nutrition that sets them up for a long, healthy, and joy-filled life. And that's where the magic of a balanced diet comes into play.

Imagine you're building a house. You wouldn't just use bricks, would you? You need cement to hold the bricks together, beams for support, windows for light, and so on. Each component serves a unique purpose, and the house wouldn't be complete or stable without all of them. Similarly, a balanced diet provides your Bullmastiff with a variety of nutrients, each with a distinct role in their overall health.

Let's consider proteins, the building blocks of your dog's body. They're vital for growth, tissue repair, immune function, and making essential hormones. Without sufficient protein, your Bullmastiff's body wouldn't function optimally, much like a house without sturdy beams.

Next up are carbohydrates. Some might view them as 'filler,' but in reality, they are a reliable source of energy for your Bullmastiff, especially for their brains. They're like the electricity that powers up the house, keeping everything running smoothly.

And then there's fat, which, despite its negative reputation, is vital for your Bullmastiff's health. It's not just about energy; fat is also needed for absorbing certain vitamins and producing essential fatty acids. It's like the insulation in the house, keeping everything comfortable and functional.

Of course, we can't forget about vitamins and minerals. From bone health to blood clotting, from wound healing to immune response, these micronutrients play crucial roles in countless bodily processes. They're like the nuts and bolts, the windows and doors, the little details that make the house complete and livable.

A balanced diet ensures that your Bullmastiff gets all these essential nutrients in the right proportions. It's not just about filling their bellies, but about nourishing their bodies. It contributes to a robust immune system, a vibrant coat, strong teeth and bones, and so much more. Plus, it plays a crucial role in preventing health issues, including obesity, heart disease, and various skin conditions.

In essence, feeding your Bullmastiff a balanced diet is about setting the foundation for a healthy life. It's about making sure that every meal they consume contributes to their strength, vitality, and happiness.

After all, our Bullmastiffs are more than just pets; they're family. And just like any family member, we want to ensure they have what they need to live their best life. So here's to balanced nutrition, the cornerstone of our Bullmastiffs' health and wellbeing.

Importance of Hydration

While we've talked a lot about food and its vital role in your Bullmastiff's health, there's another equally essential, yet sometimes overlooked, aspect of their nutrition - water. It's so simple, so basic, yet it's arguably the most important nutrient your Bullmastiff requires.

Think about how you feel on a hot summer day when you've been outside for too long. That parched feeling in your throat, the fatigue setting in, your body craving for a glass of cold water. It's a relief, isn't it? To quench your thirst, to rehydrate your body. Just as you need water to keep your body functioning and feeling good, so does your Bullmastiff.

Around 60-70% of a dog's body is made up of water, making it vital for almost every bodily function. From aiding digestion to maintaining body temperature, from helping circulate blood to facilitating waste removal, water's role in your Bullmastiff's body is as expansive as the ocean.

Hydration isn't just about quenching thirst, though. It's about maintaining a state of balance in your Bullmastiff's body. Dehydration can throw this balance off, leading to a range of health problems, from urinary tract infections to kidney diseases, from fatigue to overheating. It can even be life-threatening in severe cases.

So, how much water does your Bullmastiff need? A good rule of thumb is to offer an ounce of water per pound of body weight daily. That's around 8-10 cups of water for an average Bullmastiff. But remember, this is just a guideline. The exact amount can vary based on factors like their diet, activity level, age, and the weather. For instance, during hot summer months or after a vigorous play session, your Bullmastiff might need more water to replenish what they've lost through panting.

Providing clean, fresh water for your Bullmastiff at all times is a small act, but it's a cornerstone of their health and wellbeing. You might not see them drink often, but rest assured, they'll drink when they need to if water is readily available.

So, let's toast to hydration, an often unsung hero in your Bullmastiff's nutrition. Here's to filling up that water bowl as diligently as we fill their food dish, to monitoring their water intake, to recognizing the signs of dehydration. Because hydration, just like balanced nutrition, is key to a healthy, happy Bullmastiff.

Treats and Supplements

Ever seen the way your Bullmastiff's eyes light up when you reach for the treat jar? That eager wag of the tail, the undivided attention they suddenly have for you? Treats have a way of bringing out the joyful, playful side of your Bullmastiff, making them an essential tool for training and bonding. But there's more to treats than just being tasty morsels of joy.

Treats can also contribute to your Bullmastiff's overall nutrition when chosen wisely. They can be a way to sneak in some extra vitamins, minerals, and other nutrients that might be missing from their regular diet. That said, treats should only make up about 10% of your Bullmastiff's daily caloric intake. Any more, and you might be tipping the scales towards obesity.

When picking out treats for your Bullmastiff, keep an eye out for high-quality ingredients. Avoid treats loaded with artificial colors, flavors, or preservatives. Also, steer clear of those high in sugars and fats. Opt for natural, wholesome treats that offer nutritional benefits. For example, dental chews can help keep your Bullmastiff's teeth clean, while treats fortified with glucosamine can support joint health.

Now, let's talk about supplements. While a well-balanced diet should ideally provide all the nutrients your Bullmastiff needs, there are instances when supplements can be beneficial. For example, if your Bullmastiff has a specific health condition like arthritis, your vet might recommend a joint supplement. Or, if their diet lacks a certain nutrient, a vitamin or mineral supplement might be necessary.

However, keep in mind that not all Bullmastiffs will need supplements, and they should never be given without a vet's recommendation. Some supplements can interact with medications, while others can cause harm if given in excess. It's always best to consult with your vet before starting your Bullmastiff on any supplement.

In the grand scheme of your Bullmastiff's nutrition, treats and supplements might seem like small pieces of a big puzzle. But as we've learned, every piece counts. Treats can make learning fun, reinforce good behavior, and even offer some health benefits. And while supplements are not always necessary, they can be beneficial under the right circumstances.

So, whether it's rewarding your Bullmastiff with a healthy treat or giving them a vet-recommended supplement, remember that these little extras can contribute to their overall health and wellbeing, adding a bit more flavor and balance to their lives.

THE BULLMASTIFF

CHAPTER 6: TRAINING ESSENTIALS

Training your Bullmastiff is not just about teaching them basic commands or tricks; it's about fostering a strong bond, ensuring their safety, and shaping them into well-behaved companions. In this chapter, we will explore the essential aspects of training your Bullmastiff, from early socialization to advanced training techniques.

Socialization is a critical component of a Bullmastiff's training journey. It involves exposing them to various people, animals, and environments from a young age, helping them develop confidence and positive associations. Introduce your Bullmastiff to different sights, sounds, and experiences, gradually and positively. Socialization not only builds their ability to adapt but also helps prevent fear-based behaviors later in life.

Basic obedience training is the foundation of any well-behaved Bullmastiff. Teach them commands like "sit," "stay," "come," and "down" using positive reinforcement techniques. Reward their good behavior with treats, praise, and play. Consistency is key; practice daily in short sessions, making training a fun and engaging experience for both of you.

When it comes to managing behavioral issues, understanding the root cause is crucial. Identify any triggers or patterns that may be contributing to the problem behavior and address them accordingly. Seek professional help if needed, as a certified dog trainer or behaviorist can provide guidance tailored to your Bullmastiff's specific needs.

Advanced training can take your Bullmastiff's skills to the next level. Consider activities like agility, scent work, or obedience trials. These not only provide mental and physical stimulation but also strengthen the bond between you and your Bullmastiff. Remember, though, to always consider your dog's individual temperament, health, and energy levels when engaging in advanced training activities.

Positive reinforcement is a fundamental principle in training Bullmastiffs. Reward their desired behaviors with treats, praise, or play, rather than resorting to punishment or harsh training methods. This approach fosters a trusting and cooperative relationship, making training more enjoyable for both of you. Remember to be patient and consistent, celebrating even the smallest achievements along the way.

Housebreaking and crate training are essential for a well-adjusted Bullmastiff. Establish a routine, take them outside regularly, and reward them when they eliminate in the appropriate spot. Crate training can help with housebreaking, providing your Bullmastiff with a safe and comfortable space of their own. Gradually introduce them to the crate, associate it with positive experiences, and avoid using it as a form of punishment.

As you embark on your Bullmastiff's training journey, remember that it's a lifelong commitment. Training isn't a one-time event but an ongoing process of reinforcement and guidance. Keep your Bullmastiff mentally stimulated with puzzle toys, interactive games, and new experiences. Regularly review and reinforce their training, ensuring that the lessons stay fresh in their minds.

Above all, enjoy the training journey with your Bullmastiff. It's an opportunity for growth, learning, and creating lasting memories. Celebrate their progress, adapt to their unique personality, and remember that training is a reflection of your love and dedication to their well-being. With patience, consistency, and a whole lot of positive reinforcement, you and your Bullmastiff can achieve incredible results and forge an unbreakable bond.

The Need for Early Socialization

Imagine a world full of exciting adventures, new friends, and countless experiences. That's the world your Bullmastiff will discover through the magic of socialization. Early socialization plays a crucial role in shaping your Bullmastiff's temperament, behavior, and overall well-being. It's like laying the foundation for a lifetime of confidence and positive interactions.

The socialization journey begins as soon as you bring your Bullmastiff puppy home. During their first few weeks and months, their minds are like sponges, eagerly soaking up the sights, sounds, and smells of the world around them. This is the perfect time to expose them to a wide variety of people, animals, and environments.

Introduce your Bullmastiff to family members, friends, and neighbors, gradually expanding their circle of human companions. Encourage gentle interactions and positive experiences. Let them experience different age groups, from children to older adults, ensuring they become comfortable with people of all ages.

Socializing your Bullmastiff with other dogs is equally important. Arrange playdates with friendly, well-mannered dogs, and visit dog parks or dog-friendly areas. Observe their interactions closely, stepping in if needed, to ensure positive and appropriate behavior. Early exposure to different breeds, sizes, and energy levels will help your Bullmastiff become a well-rounded canine citizen.

Don't forget about other animals too! Introduce your Bullmastiff to cats, birds, rabbits, and other household pets, always prioritizing their safety and comfort. Monitor their reactions and provide positive reinforcement when they exhibit calm and appropriate behavior.

The world is full of sensory delights for your Bullmastiff to explore. Take them on walks in various environments, exposing them to different sounds, surfaces, and situations. Gradually introduce them to traffic, crowds, and unfamiliar places. Make these experiences positive and rewarding, using treats, toys, and praise to associate new situations with positivity.

Early socialization is not just about preventing fear-based behaviors; it's about helping your Bullmastiff develop into a confident, well-adjusted adult. Properly socialized dogs are more likely to handle stressful situations with grace, have fewer behavioral issues, and enjoy a higher quality of life.

Remember, the socialization process doesn't end when your Bullmastiff reaches a certain age. Continue exposing them to new experiences throughout their life, reinforcing their positive associations and maintaining their social skills. The more positive encounters they have, the more confident they'll become.

So, embrace the world of socialization with your Bullmastiff. Open their eyes to the wonders around them, help them build trust and understanding, and watch as they grow into a happy and socially adept companion. Together, you'll create a strong bond, filled with cherished memories and a deep sense of connection.

Training for Basic Obedience

Picture this: your Bullmastiff sits at your side, patiently waiting for your cue. With a gentle command, they gracefully lower their body into a perfect sit. You reward them with a smile, a treat, and a warm pat on the head. Ah, the beauty of basic obedience training! It's not just about impressing your friends; it's about building a strong foundation of communication and mutual understanding with your Bullmastiff.

Basic obedience training is an essential part of your Bullmastiff's education. It establishes the groundwork for good manners, cooperation, and safety. Whether you have a playful puppy or an adult Bullmastiff, it's never too late to start teaching them the basics.

Let's begin with the first command most dogs learn: "sit." It's a simple yet powerful command that teaches your Bullmastiff to control their impulse and maintain a calm demeanor. Start by holding a treat close to their nose, then slowly raise it above their head. As their gaze follows the treat, their hind end naturally lowers into a seated position. Reward them immediately with the treat and enthusiastic praise. Repeat this process until they respond consistently to the "sit" command.

"Stay" is another crucial command for your Bullmastiff's safety. Begin with your Bullmastiff in a sitting position, and with an open palm facing them, use the cue word "stay" while taking a step back. Gradually increase the distance and duration as they become more comfortable with the command.

Reward them generously when they remain in place until released. This command can be a lifesaver in potentially dangerous situations.

The recall command, "come," is vital for calling your Bullmastiff to you, no matter the circumstance. Start in a controlled environment, such as indoors or a fenced area. Crouch down, open your arms wide, and with an enthusiastic tone, call out their name followed by the command "come." When they reach you, shower them with praise, treats, and lots of affection. Gradually practice this command in different environments, reinforcing their response with positive rewards.

"Down" is another valuable command, teaching your Bullmastiff to lie down calmly on command. Begin with your Bullmastiff in a sitting position, holding a treat close to their nose. Slowly lower the treat to the ground between their paws, leading them into a down position. As soon as they lie down, reward them and offer plenty of praise. Consistency and repetition will help them understand and master this command.

Positive reinforcement is the key to effective basic obedience training. Reward your Bullmastiff's correct response with treats, verbal praise, and physical affection. Use a happy, enthusiastic tone to make training sessions enjoyable for both of you. Consistency is vital; practice these commands daily in short sessions, gradually increasing the difficulty as your Bullmastiff becomes more proficient.

Remember, training is not just about teaching commands; it's also about building a strong bond and fostering mutual trust. Take the time to understand your Bullmastiff's unique learning style, and adapt your training techniques to suit their individual needs. Patience, consistency, and a sense of humor will go a long way in creating a positive and rewarding training experience.

So, grab some tasty treats, put on your training hat, and embark on this journey of basic obedience with your Bullmastiff. Together, you'll build a solid foundation of communication, respect, and companionship that will enrich both your lives for years to come.

Managing Behavioral Issues

Just like us humans, Bullmastiffs can sometimes exhibit behavioral issues that require attention and management. From separation anxiety to leash pulling, from excessive barking to aggression, these behaviors can be challenging for both you and your beloved Bullmastiff. However, with patience, understanding, and the right approach, many behavioral issues can be effectively addressed and managed.

The first step in managing behavioral issues is to identify the root cause. Sometimes, a behavior is simply a result of your Bullmastiff's natural instincts or lack of training. Other times, it may be triggered by fear, anxiety, or past experiences. Understanding the underlying cause will guide you towards the most appropriate solution.

If you're experiencing behavioral issues with your Bullmastiff, it's important to rule out any potential medical reasons. Certain health conditions or pain can contribute to behavioral changes. Consult with your veterinarian to ensure that there are no underlying medical issues impacting your Bullmastiff's behavior. Positive reinforcement training techniques are invaluable in managing behavioral issues. Instead of resorting to punishment or dominance-based methods, focus on rewarding desired behaviors. Use treats, praise, and play to reinforce positive actions, redirecting your Bullmastiff's attention away from the problematic behavior.

Consistency is key when managing behavioral issues. Set clear boundaries and establish consistent rules. This will provide your Bullmastiff with structure and predictability, helping to alleviate confusion and reduce unwanted behaviors. Ensure that all family members are on the same page and apply consistent training techniques.

For more complex or persistent behavioral issues, consider seeking professional help from a certified dog trainer or behaviorist. These experts can assess the situation, provide personalized guidance, and develop a customized behavior modification plan. They can offer valuable insights into understanding your Bullmastiff's behavior and implementing effective training strategies.

Remember that managing behavioral issues takes time and patience. It's important to have realistic expectations and understand that progress may be gradual. Celebrate small victories along the way and stay committed to your Bullmastiff's well-being.

In some cases, managing behavioral issues may require environmental modifications. For example, if your Bullmastiff experiences separation anxiety, creating a calm and comfortable space for them when you're away can help alleviate their distress. Providing engaging toys, leaving soothing music or white noise, and gradually desensitizing them to your departures can all contribute to reducing separation anxiety.

Remember that managing behavioral issues is not about eradicating your Bullmastiff's personality or suppressing their natural instincts. It's about guiding and channeling their behaviors in a positive and appropriate direction. Be patient, understanding, and compassionate as you work together with your Bullmastiff to overcome these challenges.

By addressing and managing behavioral issues, you can help your Bullmastiff become a well-adjusted and happy companion. The journey may have its ups and downs, but with your dedication and love, you can make a positive difference in your Bullmastiff's behavior and overall quality of life.

Techniques for Advanced Training

Congratulations! You and your Bullmastiff have mastered the basics of obedience training, and now you're ready to take things to the next level with advanced training techniques. Advanced training not only challenges your Bullmastiff mentally and physically but also deepens the bond between you as you work together towards new goals. Let's explore some techniques to enhance your Bullmastiff's training repertoire.

1. **Targeting**: Teaching your Bullmastiff to target a specific object, such as your hand or a target stick, opens up a world of possibilities. This technique can be used to teach them advanced commands, tricks, or even agility maneuvers. Start by presenting the target object and rewarding your Bullmastiff for touching it with their nose or paw. Gradually shape the behavior to perform more complex actions, like following the target or touching it with different body parts.

2. **Shaping**: Shaping is a technique that involves breaking down complex behaviors into smaller, manageable steps. By rewarding your Bullmastiff for incremental progress, you can gradually shape the desired behavior. For example, if you want to teach your Bullmastiff to jump through a hoop, you would start by rewarding them for approaching the hoop, then for touching it, and eventually for going through it. Shaping encourages problem-solving skills and helps your Bullmastiff understand the desired outcome.

3. **Backchaining**: Backchaining is a technique often used in obedience trials and complex behaviors. It involves teaching your Bullmastiff the last step of a behavior sequence first and then gradually working backward. This approach helps build confidence and clarity as your Bullmastiff knows the reward is imminent at each step. For example, if you want your Bullmastiff to retrieve an item and place it in

your hand, you would first teach them to place the item in your hand, then gradually add the step of picking up the item before placing it.
4. **Capturing**: Capturing is all about seizing the moment and rewarding your Bullmastiff for naturally occurring behaviors that you want to reinforce. Observe your Bullmastiff closely and have treats or a clicker ready. When they display the desired behavior, mark it with a click or a verbal cue, and reward them immediately. For example, if you want to reinforce calm behavior, capture and reward moments of relaxation or settling down on their own. Capturing encourages your Bullmastiff to offer behaviors spontaneously.

5. **Distracted Environment Training**: As your Bullmastiff progresses in their training, it's important to expose them to increasingly distracting environments. This helps generalize their training, ensuring they respond reliably in various real-world situations. Gradually introduce distractions, such as other dogs, noises, or stimulating environments, while reinforcing their focus and obedience. Use higher-value treats and increased praise to maintain their attention amidst distractions.

Remember, advanced training requires patience, consistency, and plenty of positive reinforcement. Break down complex behaviors into achievable steps, gradually increasing the difficulty as your Bullmastiff becomes more proficient. Keep training sessions engaging and enjoyable, incorporating play and fun into the process.

Advanced training also provides an excellent opportunity for mental and physical stimulation. Engage your Bullmastiff in activities like scent work, agility, or advanced obedience trials. These activities not only challenge their abilities but also provide outlets for their natural instincts and energy.

Always be mindful of your Bullmastiff's well-being and limitations. Adjust the training to their individual needs, taking into account their age, health, and energy levels. If at any point you encounter challenges or feel overwhelmed, don't hesitate to seek guidance from a professional dog trainer or attend advanced training classes.

As you embark on the journey of advanced training with your Bullmastiff, remember to celebrate their progress and enjoy the process together. The bond between you and your Bullmastiff will strengthen as you navigate new challenges and achieve new heights. With dedication, positive reinforcement, and a sense of adventure, you'll create a training experience that enhances both your Bullmastiff's skills and your relationship.

The Role of Positive Reinforcement

Imagine learning a new skill or task. How would you feel if someone constantly criticized or punished you for every mistake you made? It would likely dampen your enthusiasm and hinder your progress. The same holds true for our Bullmastiffs. Positive reinforcement is a powerful tool in training that focuses on rewarding desired behaviors rather than punishing unwanted ones. Let's delve into the role of positive reinforcement in shaping your Bullmastiff's training journey.

Positive reinforcement is all about emphasizing and reinforcing behaviors that we want to see more of. By rewarding your Bullmastiff for good behavior, you motivate them to repeat those actions, creating a harmonious and cooperative training environment. It's like speaking a language your Bullmastiff understands, using positivity and encouragement as your main vocabulary.

One of the key advantages of positive reinforcement is that it builds a strong bond between you and your Bullmastiff. When you reward them with treats, praise, or play, they associate you with positive experiences and affection. This deepens the trust and connection between you, fostering a solid foundation for effective training.

Timing is crucial when using positive reinforcement. The reward should be given immediately after your Bullmastiff exhibits the desired behavior. This ensures they can clearly understand which action is being reinforced. For example, when teaching them to sit, reward them as soon as their bottom touches the ground. This instant reinforcement helps them make the connection between the behavior and the reward.

Rewards can take many forms, such as treats, verbal praise, petting, or a favorite toy. Each Bullmastiff has their preferences, so it's essential to identify what motivates your furry companion. Some dogs are food-motivated, while others respond more strongly to verbal praise or playtime. Experiment with different rewards to find what truly inspires and delights your Bullmastiff.

Consistency is vital when using positive reinforcement. Be clear and consistent with your cues and expectations. Use the same command or gesture each time you want your Bullmastiff to perform a behavior. This consistency helps them understand what you're asking for and reinforces the desired action.

It's important to note that positive reinforcement doesn't mean ignoring unwanted behaviors. Rather than punishing or scolding your Bullmastiff for missteps, focus on redirecting their attention to the desired behavior and rewarding them when they respond correctly. This approach helps your Bullmastiff understand what you want from them without causing fear or confusion.

Positive reinforcement is not just about training specific commands or behaviors; it's a mindset and a way of life. By consistently applying positive reinforcement techniques, you create an environment that encourages your Bullmastiff to make good choices and exhibit desirable behaviors even outside of formal training sessions. It becomes a natural part of their everyday interactions with you and the world around them.

Remember, training with positive reinforcement is not only effective but also enjoyable for both you and your Bullmastiff. It builds trust, confidence, and a positive association with training. Each success brings a sense of accomplishment and strengthens your bond.

So, grab those treats, put on a smile, and embark on your training adventures with a positive mindset. Let positive reinforcement be the guiding principle in shaping your Bullmastiff's behavior and building a harmonious relationship. Together, you'll create a world of joy, cooperation, and endless possibilities.

General Tips for Successful Training

Training your Bullmastiff is an exciting journey that requires patience, dedication, and a dash of creativity. As you embark on this adventure, it's helpful to have some general tips in mind to set you and your Bullmastiff up for success. These tips will guide you through the training process and help you create a positive and rewarding experience for both of you.

1. **Start Early**: Training should begin as early as possible, ideally when your Bullmastiff is a puppy. The earlier you start, the easier it will be to shape their behavior and instill good habits. However, remember that it's never too late to start training, even if you have an adult Bullmastiff. Consistency and patience are key regardless of your Bullmastiff's age.

2. **Keep Training Sessions Short**: Bullmastiffs have a limited attention span, especially when they're young. Keep your training sessions short and focused, typically around 10 to 15 minutes, to maintain their engagement and

prevent boredom. End each session on a positive note, rewarding them for their efforts.

3. **Be Consistent**: Consistency is paramount in training. Use the same commands, cues, and gestures consistently throughout your Bullmastiff's training. This clarity helps them understand what is expected of them and reinforces their learning. Consistency also extends to rules and boundaries in your daily interactions.

4. **Positive Reinforcement**: We've already highlighted the importance of positive reinforcement, but it's worth emphasizing again. Use treats, praise, and play to reward your Bullmastiff for desired behaviors. This positive approach motivates them to repeat those behaviors, creating a positive and cooperative training environment.

5. **Set Realistic Goals**: It's important to set realistic goals based on your Bullmastiff's individual abilities and temperament. Every Bullmastiff is unique, and progress may vary. Break down complex behaviors into smaller steps and celebrate each milestone along the way. Adjust your expectations and be patient with your Bullmastiff's learning process.

6. **Be Patient**: Patience is a virtue in dog training. Remember that learning takes time, and your Bullmastiff may not grasp a command or behavior immediately. Avoid getting frustrated or resorting to punishment. Instead, remain

calm and consistent, providing clear guidance and rewarding small steps toward the desired behavior.

7. **Make it Fun**: Training should be a positive and enjoyable experience for both you and your Bullmastiff. Incorporate play, enthusiasm, and a sense of fun into your training sessions. Use toys, games, and interactive activities to keep your Bullmastiff engaged and excited about learning. A joyful atmosphere makes training more effective and strengthens your bond.

8. **Stay Engaged**: During training sessions, it's essential to stay fully present and engaged with your Bullmastiff. Offer your undivided attention, observe their responses, and provide timely rewards and feedback. Use a warm, encouraging tone and maintain eye contact to enhance communication and reinforce your connection.

9. **Take Breaks**: Just as your Bullmastiff needs breaks during training sessions, so do you. If you or your Bullmastiff start to feel frustrated or overwhelmed, take a short break. Allow yourselves to regroup, relax, and come back to training with a fresh mindset. Remember, training is a journey, and breaks are part of the process.

10. **Seek Professional Guidance**: If you encounter specific challenges or need additional guidance, don't hesitate to seek help from a certified dog trainer or behaviorist. These professionals have expertise in understanding

canine behavior and can provide tailored strategies to address your Bullmastiff's unique needs.

By keeping these general tips in mind, you'll create an environment that supports successful training. Embrace the journey, celebrate your Bullmastiff's progress, and enjoy the process of building a strong bond and lifelong partnership. Together, you and your Bullmastiff can achieve remarkable results and create a harmonious and well-trained companion.

Training a Bullmastiff for Specific Roles

Bullmastiffs are versatile and capable dogs that can excel in various roles beyond being a loving family pet. Whether you're interested in training your Bullmastiff as a guard dog, therapy dog, or any other specialized role, it's important to approach their training with a focused and thoughtful mindset. Let's explore the training considerations for some specific roles your Bullmastiff can undertake.

1. **Guard Dog**: Bullmastiffs have a natural instinct to protect their loved ones and their territory. If you intend to train your Bullmastiff as a guard dog, it's essential to channel their protective nature in a controlled and appropriate manner. Begin with a solid foundation of obedience training, ensuring they respond reliably to commands such as "stay," "leave it," and "bark" (to alert). Gradually introduce controlled scenarios that mimic potential security challenges. Professional guidance from a certified dog

trainer experienced in guard dog training can be invaluable in this process.

2. **Therapy Dog**: Bullmastiffs, with their gentle and calm nature, can make excellent therapy dogs. These dogs bring comfort, companionship, and emotional support to individuals in hospitals, nursing homes, or other therapeutic settings. To train your Bullmastiff as a therapy dog, focus on their socialization and obedience skills. They should be comfortable around different people, including those with physical disabilities or medical equipment. Incorporate specific therapy dog training exercises, such as exposing them to various environments and practicing gentle interactions with strangers. Consider pursuing certification through a reputable therapy dog organization to ensure you meet the necessary requirements.

3. **Search and Rescue**: Bullmastiffs possess a keen sense of smell and determination, making them potentially suitable for search and rescue work. Training a Bullmastiff for this role requires specialized skills, typically involving scent detection and tracking. Seek guidance from experienced search and rescue trainers who can help you develop a training plan that builds upon your Bullmastiff's natural abilities. This may include introducing them to different scents, teaching them to follow scent trails, and exposing them to simulated search scenarios.

4. **Service Dog**: Bullmastiffs can also be trained as service dogs to assist individuals with disabilities. Service dogs are highly trained to perform specific tasks that mitigate their owner's disability. Training a Bullmastiff for this role often involves advanced obedience, public access training, and specialized tasks tailored to the individual's needs. Collaborate with a certified service dog trainer who can guide you through the training process, ensuring your Bullmastiff is equipped to support and assist their handler effectively.

5. **Sports and Competitions**: If you're interested in engaging in dog sports or competitions with your Bullmastiff, there are various options to explore. Agility, obedience trials, rally obedience, and tracking are just a few examples. Each sport requires specific training techniques and skills. Research the requirements of the sport you're interested in and find a local training club or instructor experienced in that discipline. They can guide you in training your Bullmastiff for the specific challenges and rules of the sport.

Remember, training your Bullmastiff for specialized roles requires time, dedication, and expertise. Seek professional guidance when needed, especially for more complex roles that involve specific tasks or certifications. The process may vary depending on your Bullmastiff's individual temperament, abilities, and personal suitability for the desired role.

Whatever role you choose to train your Bullmastiff for, ensure that their well-being and happiness remain a priority. Building a strong foundation of obedience, socialization, and trust is essential regardless of the role they undertake. Adapt training techniques to suit their individual needs, maintaining a positive and cooperative training environment throughout the process.

With the right training and guidance, your Bullmastiff can excel in various specialized roles, bringing joy, support, and companionship to those they interact with. Embrace the journey, set realistic goals, and celebrate each milestone along the way. Together, you and your Bullmastiff can make a positive impact in the lives of others while deepening your bond as a remarkable team.

Housebreaking and Crate Training

Ah, the joys of a clean and well-maintained home! Housebreaking your Bullmastiff is an essential part of their training journey. Teaching them appropriate bathroom habits and crate training can help create a harmonious living environment for both you and your furry friend. Let's explore some tips and techniques for successful housebreaking and crate training.

Housebreaking your Bullmastiff begins with establishing a consistent routine. Take your Bullmastiff outside to their designated bathroom spot at regular intervals throughout the day, especially after meals, naps, playtime, or waking up. Give them ample time to relieve themselves and reward them immediately when they do so in the appropriate location. Positive reinforcement, such as treats, praise, and a cheerful tone, helps them associate going potty outside with positive outcomes.

Keep a close eye on your Bullmastiff, especially during the housebreaking process. Watch for signs that they need to eliminate, such as sniffing, circling, or restlessness. If you notice these signs, quickly and calmly guide them to the designated bathroom spot.

If accidents happen indoors, avoid scolding or punishing your Bullmastiff, as this can create fear or confusion. Instead, focus on reinforcing good habits and redirecting them to the appropriate location. Crate training can be a valuable tool in housebreaking and providing a safe space for your Bullmastiff.

Choose a crate that is spacious enough for them to stand, turn around, and lie down comfortably. Make the crate inviting with soft bedding and toys. Introduce the crate gradually, allowing your Bullmastiff to explore it at their own pace. Use positive reinforcement to create positive associations with the crate, such as offering treats and praise when they enter voluntarily.

When using the crate for housebreaking, follow a schedule that includes supervised crate time, playtime, potty breaks, and periods of relaxation outside the crate. A general rule of thumb is that puppies can hold their bladder for approximately one hour per month of age. Adjust the timing accordingly, ensuring your Bullmastiff gets frequent potty breaks to avoid accidents.

Never use the crate as a form of punishment. The crate should be a safe and comfortable space where your Bullmastiff can relax and retreat when needed. Avoid leaving them in the crate for excessive periods of time, as this can lead to boredom or anxiety. Gradually increase the duration of crate time as your Bullmastiff becomes more comfortable and reliable with their housebreaking routine.

Consistency and patience are key in housebreaking and crate training. Remember that accidents may happen, especially during the early stages. Stay positive and continue reinforcing good habits. Over time, your Bullmastiff will develop bladder control, understand the designated bathroom spot, and become reliable in their housebreaking routine.

It's important to note that housebreaking and crate training may take several weeks or even months, depending on your Bullmastiff's individual learning pace. Be patient and remain consistent in your approach. Celebrate each successful potty break outside and provide gentle guidance when accidents occur.

As your Bullmastiff progresses in their housebreaking and crate training, gradually give them more freedom and access to different areas of the house. Always supervise them until you're confident in their ability to consistently follow the house rules. With time, consistency, and positive reinforcement, your Bullmastiff will become a well-mannered and reliable companion within your home.

So, embrace the adventure of housebreaking and crate training with your Bullmastiff. Create a routine, be patient, and reinforce good habits. Soon enough, you'll enjoy the benefits of a happy, well-behaved Bullmastiff and a clean, peaceful home.

CHAPTER 7: EXERCISE AND MENTAL STIMULATION

Exercise and mental stimulation are vital for the overall well-being and happiness of your Bullmastiff. As an energetic and intelligent breed, Bullmastiffs require regular physical activity and mental engagement to thrive. In this chapter, we'll delve into the importance of exercise and mental stimulation, providing you with practical tips to keep your Bullmastiff physically and mentally stimulated.

Exercise is not only essential for keeping your Bullmastiff physically fit but also helps to maintain their mental and emotional well-being. Regular exercise helps prevent obesity, strengthens muscles, improves cardiovascular health, and promotes overall vitality. It also provides an outlet for their energy, reducing the likelihood of behavioral problems caused by pent-up energy.

The exercise needs of your Bullmastiff will vary depending on their age, health, and individual energy levels. As a general guideline, adult Bullmastiffs typically benefit from at least 30 minutes to one hour of exercise per day. Puppies and young Bullmastiffs may require more frequent exercise sessions, taking their growing bodies into consideration.

Tailor your Bullmastiff's exercise routine to their specific needs. Activities such as brisk walks, jogging, or hiking can help burn off excess energy while keeping them physically stimulated. Off-leash playtime in a safely enclosed area or dog park can provide opportunities for socialization and running around. Engaging in canine sports, such as agility or obedience trials, can also provide mental and physical challenges for your Bullmastiff.

In addition to physical exercise, mental stimulation is crucial for preventing boredom and keeping your Bullmastiff's mind sharp. Mental stimulation helps ward off destructive behaviors that may arise from boredom and provides an outlet for their natural curiosity and problem-solving abilities. Incorporating mental exercises into your Bullmastiff's routine can be as important as physical exercise.

There are several ways to provide mental stimulation for your Bullmastiff. Interactive puzzle toys or treat-dispensing toys can keep their minds engaged as they figure out how to access the treats. Hide-and-seek games, where you hide treats or toys around the house or yard, tap into their natural scenting abilities and provide a fun and rewarding challenge.

Training sessions can also serve as a valuable mental workout for your Bullmastiff. Teach them new commands or tricks, and engage in obedience training to keep their minds active and focused. This not only strengthens the bond between you but also provides mental stimulation as they learn and respond to different cues.

Consider introducing your Bullmastiff to scent work or nose games. These activities tap into their exceptional sense of smell, allowing them to engage in a natural and mentally stimulating task. You can start by hiding treats or toys and gradually increase the difficulty by using different scents or creating scent trails for them to follow.

Remember that mental stimulation should be varied and challenging. Rotate toys, activities, and training exercises to keep your Bullmastiff's mind engaged and prevent boredom. Keep sessions short and enjoyable, ending on a positive note to keep them eager for more.

When planning exercise and mental stimulation for your Bullmastiff, consider their individual needs and limitations. Take into account their age, any health concerns, and the current weather conditions. Be cautious not to overexert them, especially in extreme temperatures or if they have certain health conditions that require modifications to their exercise routine.

By providing regular exercise and mental stimulation, you're not only promoting your Bullmastiff's physical and mental well-being but also strengthening the bond between you. The time spent engaging in activities together allows for quality bonding experiences and reinforces your role as their trusted companion.

So, get ready for enjoyable walks, engaging training sessions, and exciting mental challenges with your Bullmastiff. Tailor their exercise routine to their individual needs, stay consistent, and always prioritize their safety and well-being. With a well-rounded approach to exercise and mental stimulation, you'll have a happy, healthy, and contented Bullmastiff by your side.

Exercise Requirements

One of the keys to keeping your Bullmastiff healthy and happy is ensuring they receive adequate exercise. Bullmastiffs are a breed known for their strength and endurance, and regular exercise is essential to maintain their physical well-being. In this section, we'll delve into the exercise requirements for Bullmastiffs, providing you with guidelines to keep them fit and thriving.

As a guardian breed with a moderate activity level, Bullmastiffs benefit from regular exercise to keep their muscles toned, prevent obesity, and promote overall vitality. However, it's important to consider their specific needs and adjust their exercise routine accordingly. While Bullmastiffs require exercise, they are not as high-energy as some other breeds.

Aim for a minimum of 30 minutes to one hour of exercise per day for adult Bullmastiffs. This can be split into two or more sessions to accommodate their individual energy levels and avoid excessive strain. Puppies and young Bullmastiffs may require shorter but more frequent exercise sessions to prevent overexertion and accommodate their growing bodies.

One of the simplest and most enjoyable forms of exercise for your Bullmastiff is walking. Daily walks provide an opportunity for them to explore their surroundings, get fresh air, and engage in light physical activity. Aim for a brisk pace to ensure they receive the appropriate level of exercise. Gradually increase the duration and intensity of the walks as your Bullmastiff's fitness improves.

In addition to regular walks, consider incorporating other forms of exercise to keep your Bullmastiff engaged. Jogging or running alongside a bicycle can provide a more vigorous workout, catering to their higher energy levels. However, be cautious and introduce these activities gradually, allowing their bodies to adjust and avoiding excessive strain.

Off-leash playtime in a safely enclosed area or a dog park allows your Bullmastiff to socialize, interact with other dogs, and run freely. These activities not only provide physical exercise but also mental stimulation and an outlet for their natural playfulness. Always supervise off-leash play and ensure the area is secure and suitable for your Bullmastiff's size and temperament.

Swimming can be an excellent low-impact exercise option for Bullmastiffs, particularly during hot weather. Many Bullmastiffs naturally enjoy the water and find swimming to be a refreshing and enjoyable activity. If you have access to a safe swimming area, allow your Bullmastiff to take a dip and have fun while exercising their muscles.

While exercise is important, it's crucial to be mindful of your Bullmastiff's limitations. They are a brachycephalic breed, meaning they have a shortened muzzle, which can affect their ability to regulate body temperature efficiently. Avoid exercising them excessively in extreme heat or humidity to prevent overheating. Provide plenty of fresh water and choose cooler times of the day for outdoor activities.

It's also important to tailor the exercise routine to your Bullmastiff's individual needs. Some Bullmastiffs may have higher energy levels and require more intense exercise, while others may be more laid-back and prefer a moderate pace. Pay attention to their cues, observe their energy levels, and adjust the duration and intensity of exercise accordingly.

Remember that exercise should be enjoyable for both you and your Bullmastiff. It's an opportunity to bond, explore the world together, and promote their overall well-being. Be present, engage with them during exercise, and make it a positive experience filled with praise, rewards, and quality time together.

By providing regular exercise that aligns with their needs, you'll help your Bullmastiff maintain a healthy weight, prevent boredom-related behaviors, and promote their overall fitness. So, grab the leash, put on your walking shoes, and embark on the adventure of keeping your Bullmastiff active and content.

Suitable Sports and Activities

In addition to regular walks and playtime, engaging your Bullmastiff in sports and specific activities can provide them with additional mental and physical stimulation. These activities allow your Bullmastiff to showcase their natural abilities, bond with you, and explore new challenges. Let's explore some suitable sports and activities that are well-suited for Bullmastiffs.

1. **Agility**: Agility is a popular canine sport that involves navigating an obstacle course comprising jumps, tunnels, weave poles, and more. Bullmastiffs, despite their size, can participate in agility and excel with proper training and guidance. This sport not only tests their physical agility but also requires mental focus and teamwork with their handler. It's a great way to build confidence, enhance obedience skills, and provide a fun and challenging outlet for their energy.

2. **Obedience Trials**: Obedience trials are competitions that assess a dog's ability to follow commands and demonstrate good manners. These trials typically include various obedience exercises, such as heeling, recalls, stays, and more. Bullmastiffs, known for their calm and obedient nature, can excel in obedience trials. Participating in these events not only provides mental stimulation but also strengthens the bond between you and your

Bullmastiff as you work together to achieve success.

3. **Rally Obedience**: Rally obedience combines elements of traditional obedience with a more interactive and dynamic approach. In rally obedience, you and your Bullmastiff navigate a course, following a series of signs that indicate different exercises to perform. This sport emphasizes teamwork, focus, and precise execution of commands. It's an enjoyable and mentally stimulating activity that allows you to showcase your Bullmastiff's skills while building a strong partnership.

4. **Tracking**: Bullmastiffs possess an exceptional sense of smell, making them well-suited for tracking activities. Tracking involves following a scent trail to locate specific objects or individuals. Engaging in tracking exercises taps into your Bullmastiff's natural instincts and provides a mentally challenging and rewarding activity. It's an excellent way to channel their scenting abilities and engage in a fulfilling task that stimulates their minds.

5. **Weight Pulling**: Weight pulling is a sport that tests a dog's strength and pulling ability. Bullmastiffs, with their impressive muscular build, can participate in weight pulling events. In this sport, your Bullmastiff is harnessed to a sled or cart loaded with weights, and they pull it over a set distance. Weight pulling helps develop their muscles, provides an outlet for

6. **Swimming**: Swimming is not only a fun and low-impact exercise but also a suitable activity for Bullmastiffs. Many Bullmastiffs enjoy the water and are natural swimmers. Swimming helps build their muscles, provides a refreshing way to cool down during hot weather, and offers an opportunity for mental and physical stimulation. Ensure that swimming takes place in safe and controlled environments, such as pools or designated swimming areas, and always supervise your Bullmastiff while they swim.

These are just a few examples of sports and activities that can be suitable for Bullmastiffs. It's essential to consider your Bullmastiff's individual strengths, abilities, and interests when choosing an activity. Some Bullmastiffs may excel in one sport while showing less enthusiasm for another. Listen to your Bullmastiff's preferences and capabilities, and adjust accordingly to provide them with an enjoyable and rewarding experience.

Participating in sports and activities with your Bullmastiff is not only beneficial for their physical and mental well-being but also strengthens the bond between you. These shared experiences promote teamwork, trust, and a sense of accomplishment. Always prioritize safety, provide appropriate training, and consult with professionals or experienced trainers to ensure you engage in activities suitable for your Bullmastiff's age, fitness level, and health.

So, explore the world of canine sports and activities, find what resonates with your Bullmastiff's abilities, and embark on exciting adventures together. Whether it's navigating an agility course, demonstrating obedience skills, engaging in tracking exercises, or enjoying a swim, these activities will bring joy, fulfillment, and a stronger bond between you and your Bullmastiff.

Mental Exercise and Enrichment

In addition to physical exercise, providing mental exercise and enrichment is essential for the well-being of your Bullmastiff. Mental stimulation keeps their minds sharp, prevents boredom, and contributes to their overall happiness. Let's explore various ways to provide mental exercise and enrichment for your Bullmastiff, ensuring they lead a fulfilling and engaging life.

One of the simplest ways to provide mental exercise is through interactive playtime. Engage your Bullmastiff in games that challenge their problem-solving abilities, such as hide-and-seek or treasure hunt. Hide treats or toys around the house and encourage your Bullmastiff to find them using their sense of smell. This stimulates their natural instincts and provides a rewarding mental workout.

Training sessions are not only beneficial for teaching obedience and tricks but also for mental stimulation. Dogs love learning new things, and training engages their minds. Teach your Bullmastiff new commands, practice existing ones, and introduce fun tricks that require them to think and problem-solve. Break training into short, enjoyable sessions using positive reinforcement, making it a positive and stimulating experience.

Puzzle toys are another fantastic way to challenge your Bullmastiff's cognitive skills. These toys are designed to hide treats or require problem-solving to access rewards. By manipulating the toy, your Bullmastiff must figure out how to obtain the treats, stimulating their minds and keeping them engaged. Choose puzzle toys of appropriate difficulty and supervise their playtime.
Scent work is an activity that harnesses your Bullmastiff's exceptional sense of smell. Introduce scent-based games where they must locate hidden treats or toys using their nose. Start with simple hiding spots and gradually increase the difficulty level. Scent work engages their natural instincts, encourages mental focus, and provides a rewarding and enriching experience.

Regularly rotate and introduce new toys to keep your Bullmastiff mentally stimulated. Offering a variety of toys with different textures, shapes, and interactive features prevents boredom and keeps their interest piqued. You can also incorporate food-dispensing toys that require your Bullmastiff to work for their meals. These toys provide mental stimulation as they figure out how to access the food.

Environmental enrichment is another aspect of mental exercise. Create an engaging living environment for your Bullmastiff by introducing new sights, sounds, and experiences. Take them on different walking routes, visit new places, and expose them to various situations and environments. This helps them adapt to new experiences, keeps their minds sharp, and prevents them from becoming overly accustomed to routine.

Remember, mental exercise should be enjoyable and engaging. Pay attention to your Bullmastiff's individual preferences and adapt activities to suit their personality. Some Bullmastiffs may prefer problem-solving toys, while others may thrive on scent-based games or training exercises. Observe their reactions and adjust accordingly.

It's important to note that mental exercise should be balanced with physical exercise to maintain your Bullmastiff's overall well-being. Combining mental and physical activities ensures they lead a healthy and enriched life. As a responsible owner, make time each day to engage your Bullmastiff's mind and provide opportunities for mental stimulation and enrichment.

By incorporating mental exercise into their routine, you'll help keep their minds sharp, prevent boredom-related behaviors, and strengthen the bond between you and your Bullmastiff. So, get creative, have fun, and watch your Bullmastiff thrive as they engage in stimulating activities that challenge their minds.

Exercise as a Tool for Behavior Management

Exercise not only benefits your Bullmastiff's physical health but also plays a vital role in behavior management. Regular exercise helps channel their energy, promotes mental well-being, and reduces the likelihood of behavioral problems arising from boredom or excess energy. In this section, we'll explore how exercise can be used as a tool for behavior management and promote a well-balanced and well-behaved Bullmastiff.

Adequate exercise is key to preventing behavior problems in Bullmastiffs. These dogs have a natural inclination for guarding and protective behaviors, and when their energy isn't properly channeled, it can manifest as destructive chewing, excessive barking, or even aggression. Providing them with sufficient exercise helps to dissipate their energy and prevents these negative behaviors from arising.

Exercise is a powerful outlet for your Bullmastiff's physical and mental energy. Engaging them in regular physical activities such as walks, playtime, or interactive games helps burn off excess energy and reduces the likelihood of restlessness or hyperactivity. A tired Bullmastiff is more likely to exhibit calm and relaxed behavior, making them easier to manage.

When it comes to behavior management, consistency is key. Establishing a routine that incorporates daily exercise ensures that your Bullmastiff receives the physical and mental stimulation they need on a consistent basis. Aim for a minimum of 30 minutes to one hour of exercise per day, but adjust the duration and intensity based on their age, energy level, and overall health.

Exercise provides an opportunity for your Bullmastiff to release pent-up energy and focus their attention on constructive activities. For example, engaging them in training exercises during walks or playtime can help redirect their energy towards learning and following commands. This not only provides mental stimulation but also reinforces positive behaviors and strengthens the bond between you and your Bullmastiff.

Another benefit of exercise is that it promotes socialization and positive interactions with other dogs and people. Regular outings to dog parks, group walks, or obedience classes allow your Bullmastiff to socialize in a controlled environment. Positive social experiences help them develop good manners, build confidence, and reduce the likelihood of fear or aggression towards unfamiliar situations or individuals.

Consistent exercise also contributes to a healthier and more balanced emotional state in your Bullmastiff. Regular physical activity stimulates the release of endorphins, which are natural mood-enhancing chemicals. This can have a positive impact on their overall temperament, reducing anxiety, stress, or frustration that may contribute to undesirable behaviors.

It's important to tailor the type and intensity of exercise to your Bullmastiff's individual needs. While some Bullmastiffs may enjoy more vigorous activities like jogging or hiking, others may prefer moderate exercise such as brisk walks or gentle play. Observe your Bullmastiff's response to different activities and adjust accordingly to provide them with the appropriate level of exercise.

Remember to consider any breed-specific restrictions or health concerns when designing an exercise routine. For example, Bullmastiffs are a brachycephalic breed and can be more susceptible to heat exhaustion, so it's important to exercise them during cooler parts of the day and provide plenty of water breaks.

By incorporating regular exercise into your Bullmastiff's routine, you'll not only promote their physical health but also enhance their mental well-being and behavior. Consistent exercise helps channel their energy, reduce boredom-related behaviors, and create a calmer and more contented Bullmastiff.

So, make exercise a priority and enjoy the benefits of a well-behaved and fulfilled Bullmastiff. Whether it's a leisurely walk, a lively game of fetch, or an engaging training session, investing time in exercise will contribute to a harmonious and enjoyable life with your beloved Bullmastiff.

Exercise Routines for Different Life Stages

As your Bullmastiff progresses through different life stages, their exercise needs and capabilities will change. It's essential to adapt their exercise routines to accommodate their age, physical development, and overall health. In this section, we'll discuss exercise routines for different life stages of your Bullmastiff, ensuring they receive appropriate physical activity at every stage of their life.

Puppy Stage: During the puppy stage, exercise should be approached with caution as their bones, muscles, and joints are still developing. While it's important to provide them with opportunities for physical activity, it's equally vital to prevent overexertion or excessive impact on their growing bodies. Short and controlled play sessions, gentle walks, and interactive games that encourage mental stimulation are ideal for young Bullmastiffs. Aim for multiple short exercise sessions throughout the day to prevent exhaustion.

Adolescent Stage: As your Bullmastiff transitions into adolescence, their energy levels increase, and they require more exercise to burn off excess energy. Increase the duration and intensity of their exercise gradually, allowing them to adjust to the added physical demands. Engage in longer walks, more vigorous play sessions, and introduce structured training exercises to channel their energy and promote mental stimulation. Keep in mind that their bones and joints are still developing, so avoid excessive impact or jumping activities that could cause injury.

Adult Stage: During adulthood, your Bullmastiff will require regular exercise to maintain their physical and mental well-being. Aim for a minimum of 30 minutes to one hour of exercise per day, depending on their individual energy level and health. Brisk walks, jogging, off-leash playtime, and engaging in dog sports such as agility or obedience trials can provide the necessary physical and mental stimulation. Be attentive to any signs of fatigue or discomfort, and adjust the exercise routine accordingly.

Senior Stage: As your Bullmastiff enters their senior years, their exercise requirements will decrease, but they still benefit from regular physical activity. However, it's important to be mindful of any age-related conditions such as arthritis or reduced mobility. Adjust the exercise routine to low-impact activities that are gentle on their joints, such as leisurely walks or swimming. Shorter, more frequent exercise sessions may be more suitable for their stamina. Consult with your veterinarian to determine the appropriate exercise routine based on their individual health and limitations.

Individual Considerations: Keep in mind that each Bullmastiff is unique, and their exercise needs may vary based on factors such as their energy level, overall health, and individual preferences. Some Bullmastiffs may have lower energy levels and require less exercise, while others may have higher energy and benefit from more vigorous activities. Observe their response to exercise, monitor their stamina, and adjust accordingly to provide the appropriate level of physical activity for your Bullmastiff.

Regardless of their life stage, always prioritize their safety and well-being during exercise. Consider the weather conditions and avoid exercising in extreme heat or cold. Provide ample water breaks and monitor their breathing and overall comfort during exercise. Regular veterinary check-ups can help identify any underlying health issues that may affect their exercise routine.

Remember, exercise is not only about physical activity but also mental stimulation and bonding time with your Bullmastiff. Engage in activities that challenge their minds, encourage socialization, and provide opportunities for you to strengthen your bond. Be attentive to their needs, listen to their cues, and adjust their exercise routine as necessary.

By adapting the exercise routine to suit your Bullmastiff's life stage, you'll ensure they receive the appropriate amount of physical activity, maintain their overall health, and enjoy a well-balanced and fulfilling life. So, continue to provide them with the exercise they need at each stage of their life and watch your Bullmastiff thrive in their physical and mental well-being.

Possible Health Issues Due to Improper Exercise

While exercise is crucial for the well-being of your Bullmastiff, it's important to understand that improper exercise can lead to various health issues. Overexertion, inappropriate activities, or excessive impact can put unnecessary strain on their bodies and potentially lead to injuries or other complications. In this section, we'll explore the possible health issues that can arise due to improper exercise and how to prevent them.

One common health concern associated with improper exercise is joint and musculoskeletal problems. Bullmastiffs are a large and heavy breed, and excessive impact or intense exercise at a young age can place undue stress on their developing bones and joints. This can lead to conditions such as hip or elbow dysplasia, where the joint structures do not develop properly, resulting in discomfort, lameness, and long-term mobility issues. It's crucial to provide controlled exercise and avoid activities that involve excessive jumping or twisting, especially during their puppy and adolescent stages when their bodies are still growing.

Another health issue that can arise from improper exercise is ligament and tendon injuries. The sudden or excessive stress placed on their joints during vigorous activities can lead to strains, sprains, or even tears in the ligaments or tendons. Common examples include cruciate ligament tears, which can cause significant pain and mobility problems. It's important to gradually increase the intensity of exercise, provide appropriate warm-up and cool-down periods, and avoid sudden or excessive movements that can strain their joints and soft tissues.

Overexertion and heat-related issues are also a concern, particularly in warmer climates or during hot weather. Bullmastiffs are susceptible to heat exhaustion and heatstroke due to their brachycephalic (short-nosed) anatomy, which affects their ability to regulate body temperature efficiently. Avoid exercising them during the hottest parts of the day, provide ample water breaks, and ensure they have access to shade. Be mindful of their breathing and overall comfort during exercise, as excessive panting, drooling, or sluggishness can be signs of overheating.

Furthermore, improper exercise can exacerbate existing health conditions. For example, Bullmastiffs are prone to certain respiratory conditions, such as brachycephalic airway syndrome. Intense exercise or strenuous activities can further strain their respiratory system, leading to breathing difficulties and potential respiratory distress. It's crucial to be aware of their limitations and avoid activities that place excessive strain on their breathing.

To prevent these health issues, it's essential to create an exercise routine that considers your Bullmastiff's age, physical condition, and breed-specific characteristics. Gradually increase the intensity and duration of exercise, allowing their bodies to adapt and strengthen over time. Choose activities that are appropriate for their size and energy level, avoiding excessive impact or high-risk movements. Regular veterinary check-ups can also help identify any underlying health conditions and guide you in tailoring the exercise routine to their specific needs.

Additionally, always pay attention to your Bullmastiff's signals and body language during exercise. If they appear tired, are struggling to keep up, or show signs of discomfort, it's important to provide rest and reassess the intensity and duration of their exercise. Every Bullmastiff is unique, and their exercise requirements may vary. Some may thrive with moderate exercise, while others may have higher energy levels and require more vigorous activities. Observe their response to different exercises, monitor their stamina, and adjust accordingly to ensure their well-being.

Remember, exercise should be enjoyable and beneficial for your Bullmastiff, promoting their overall health and happiness. By providing appropriate exercise and avoiding improper activities, you'll minimize the risk of health issues and ensure a long and active life for your beloved Bullmastiff companion.

So, prioritize their well-being, be mindful of their exercise routine, and enjoy the benefits of a healthy and thriving Bullmastiff.

The Role of Play in Exercise

Play is a vital component of exercise for your Bullmastiff. It not only provides physical activity but also contributes to their mental well-being and strengthens the bond between you and your furry companion. Playtime allows them to express their natural instincts, release pent-up energy, and enjoy a joyful and fulfilling experience. In this section, we'll explore the importance of play in exercise and how it enhances your Bullmastiff's overall well-being.

Play is a natural behavior for dogs, and it serves multiple purposes in their lives. When it comes to exercise, playtime allows your Bullmastiff to engage in activities that are both physically and mentally stimulating. It provides an outlet for their energy and helps prevent boredom-related behaviors that may arise from a lack of stimulation. By incorporating play into their exercise routine, you'll create a fun and rewarding experience for your Bullmastiff.

One of the main benefits of play is that it promotes physical activity. Whether it's chasing a ball, playing tug-of-war, or engaging in interactive games, playtime gets your Bullmastiff moving, running, and jumping. This physical exertion helps burn off excess energy and contributes to their overall fitness and well-being.

Regular play sessions can help maintain a healthy weight, improve cardiovascular health, and keep their muscles strong and supple.

In addition to physical exercise, play provides mental stimulation for your Bullmastiff. Interactive games and toys challenge their problem-solving skills, engage their senses, and encourage them to think and strategize. For example, playing hide-and-seek with treats or toys stimulates their natural instincts, engages their sense of smell, and promotes mental agility as they search for hidden items. This mental engagement is just as important as physical exercise and helps keep their minds sharp and active.

Play also fosters a strong bond between you and your Bullmastiff. When you actively participate in playtime, you're not just providing exercise; you're also creating opportunities for quality time and connection. Engaging in play strengthens the emotional bond and mutual trust between you and your Bullmastiff. It's a chance to communicate, have fun, and build a positive and enjoyable relationship.

The type of play you engage in with your Bullmastiff will depend on their preferences and individual characteristics. Some Bullmastiffs enjoy chasing and retrieving toys, while others may prefer interactive games that involve problem-solving or using their senses. Observe their interests and adapt the play activities accordingly. It's important to provide a variety of play options to keep them engaged and prevent boredom.

Safety should always be a priority during playtime. Choose toys that are suitable for their size and durability, ensuring they cannot be easily ingested or cause harm. Avoid rough play that may lead to injuries, and be mindful of their energy levels and overall comfort during play. Regularly inspect toys for any signs of wear or damage, and replace them as needed.

Play should be a part of your Bullmastiff's daily routine. Incorporate short and frequent play sessions throughout the day, allowing them to release energy and engage in stimulating activities. Whether it's a game of fetch in the park, a gentle wrestling session, or interactive puzzle toys, make playtime a regular and enjoyable part of their exercise routine.

In conclusion, play is an integral aspect of exercise for your Bullmastiff. It provides physical activity, mental stimulation, and strengthens the bond between you and your furry friend. By incorporating play into their routine, you'll not only enhance their physical and mental well-being but also create a positive and rewarding experience for both of you. So, get ready to have fun, engage in play, and enjoy the many benefits it brings to your Bullmastiff's life.

CHAPTER 8: GROOMING YOUR BULLMASTIFF

Grooming is an essential aspect of caring for your Bullmastiff. It not only keeps them looking their best but also plays a crucial role in maintaining their overall health and well-being. In this chapter, we will delve into the various aspects of grooming your Bullmastiff, including bathing, coat care, dental hygiene, nail trimming, and routine health checks at home.

Bathing your Bullmastiff is an important part of their grooming routine. While they have a short coat that doesn't require frequent bathing, regular baths help keep their skin clean, remove dirt and odors, and maintain their overall hygiene. Use a mild dog shampoo formulated for sensitive skin or specifically designed for Bullmastiffs. Remember to rinse them thoroughly to ensure no soap residue remains, as this can cause skin irritation. After bathing, make sure to dry them thoroughly to prevent any moisture-related skin issues.

Coat care is crucial in keeping your Bullmastiff's coat healthy and lustrous. Despite having a short coat, regular brushing is necessary to remove loose hair and prevent matting. Use a soft-bristle brush or a grooming mitt to brush them at least once a week. This not only helps keep their coat clean and tangle-free but also provides an opportunity to check their skin for any abnormalities, such as rashes, irritations, or signs of parasites. Pay close attention to areas with skin folds, like the face, neck, and tail, as these areas require extra care to prevent moisture accumulation and potential skin problems.

Dental care is often overlooked but is a vital part of grooming your Bullmastiff. Regular brushing of their teeth helps prevent dental issues such as tartar buildup, gum disease, and bad breath. Use a dog-specific toothbrush and toothpaste to gently brush their teeth two to three times a week. Introduce tooth brushing gradually, starting with short sessions and gradually increasing the duration as they become more comfortable. In addition to brushing, consider providing dental chews or toys to help maintain their oral hygiene.

Nail trimming is an essential grooming task for your Bullmastiff. Overgrown nails can be uncomfortable for them and may affect their gait. Use a dog-specific nail clipper or grinder to trim their nails, being cautious not to cut into the quick, which is the sensitive part of the nail that contains blood vessels and nerves. If you're unsure about how to trim their nails safely, seek guidance from a professional groomer or veterinarian. Regular nail trimming, typically every four to six weeks, helps keep their paws in good condition and prevents potential nail-related issues.

Routine health checks at home are an integral part of grooming your Bullmastiff. Regularly inspect their ears, eyes, teeth, skin, and overall body condition. Look for any signs of redness, discharge, swelling, or abnormalities. Check their ears for excessive wax buildup or signs of infection, and gently clean them with a dog-specific ear cleaner if necessary. Examine their eyes for any redness, discharge, or cloudiness, and consult your veterinarian if you notice any issues. Regularly inspect their teeth and gums for signs of dental problems, such as inflammation or tartar buildup. By conducting these routine checks, you can detect potential health issues early and seek appropriate veterinary care if needed.

Addressing common grooming issues is an essential part of keeping your Bullmastiff comfortable and healthy. Some Bullmastiffs may experience skin conditions such as allergies or hot spots. Regular grooming, including brushing, bathing with appropriate products, and maintaining a clean and dry environment, can help prevent and manage these issues. Shedding is a natural process for Bullmastiffs, particularly during seasonal changes. Regular brushing helps remove loose hair and keeps shedding under control. Additionally, keep an eye out for any signs of parasites, such as fleas or ticks, and take appropriate measures to prevent and treat infestations.

Grooming your Bullmastiff is not just about maintaining their physical appearance; it's about promoting their overall health and well-being. Regular grooming sessions provide an opportunity to bond with your furry companion, monitor their condition, and address any concerns promptly. Remember to approach grooming with patience, positivity, and a gentle touch. Your Bullmastiff will appreciate the care and attention, and you'll enjoy a clean, healthy, and happy canine companion as a result.

Bathing and Coat Care

Bathing and coat care are essential aspects of grooming your Bullmastiff. Regular bathing keeps their skin clean, removes dirt and odors, and helps maintain their overall hygiene. Additionally, proper coat care ensures that their fur remains healthy, shiny, and free from tangles or matting. In this section, we'll explore the best practices for bathing and coat care to keep your Bullmastiff looking and feeling their best.

Bathing your Bullmastiff should be done at regular intervals, but not too frequently as it can strip their skin of natural oils. Generally, bathing them once every two to three months is sufficient unless they get particularly dirty or smelly. However, always adapt the bathing frequency based on your Bullmastiff's specific needs and activities. For example, if they love playing in muddy puddles or rolling in something unpleasant, you may need to bathe them more often.

When it's time for a bath, ensure that you use a mild dog shampoo specifically formulated for Bullmastiffs or dogs with sensitive skin. Avoid using human shampoos or harsh products that can irritate their skin. Wet their coat thoroughly with warm water, taking care to avoid getting water in their ears and eyes. Apply the shampoo and lather it gently, massaging it into their coat. Be thorough but avoid excessive rubbing or scrubbing, as it can cause skin irritation.

Rinse your Bullmastiff thoroughly, ensuring that no shampoo residue remains on their skin or coat. Leftover shampoo can lead to skin dryness or irritation. Rinse until the water runs clear, and there are no traces of suds. Take extra care to rinse the areas where their skin folds, such as around the face, neck, and tail, as these areas can trap shampoo if not rinsed properly.

After bathing, gently towel-dry your Bullmastiff, being careful not to rub too vigorously. Their dense coat can take a while to dry completely, so ensure that they are kept in a warm and draft-free environment until they are fully dry. Avoid exposing them to cold or damp conditions immediately after bathing, as it can lead to discomfort or even illness. If needed, you can use a low-heat blow dryer on the lowest setting to aid in the drying process. However, always keep the dryer at a safe distance from their skin to prevent burns or discomfort.

Coat care between baths is equally important in maintaining your Bullmastiff's coat health. Regular brushing helps remove loose hair, distribute natural oils, and prevent tangles or matting. Use a soft-bristle brush or a grooming mitt to brush their coat at least once a week. Start at the head and work your way down, being gentle and thorough in your strokes. Pay close attention to areas where their coat is thicker or prone to matting, such as the neck, chest, and hindquarters.

During the brushing session, take the opportunity to check their skin for any signs of irritation, redness, or parasites. If you notice any abnormalities or suspect the presence of fleas or ticks, consult your veterinarian for appropriate treatment. Regular brushing not only helps maintain their coat health but also provides a bonding experience and allows you to monitor their overall well-being.

In addition to regular brushing, be proactive in addressing any skin issues or concerns promptly. Bullmastiffs are prone to certain skin conditions, such as allergies or hot spots, which may require specific care. If you notice any signs of itching, redness, inflammation, or persistent skin problems, consult your veterinarian for guidance. They can recommend appropriate treatments, shampoos, or dietary changes to help alleviate the issue.

Remember that proper bathing and coat care go beyond physical hygiene. They are also opportunities to bond with your Bullmastiff and show them love and care. Approach grooming with patience, kindness, and a gentle touch. Make it a positive experience for both of you, and soon enough, your Bullmastiff will come to enjoy the attention and pampering that grooming provides.

In conclusion, bathing and coat care are essential for keeping your Bullmastiff clean, healthy, and comfortable. By following the recommended bathing schedule, using appropriate products, and practicing regular brushing, you'll help maintain their skin and coat in optimal condition. Enjoy the bonding moments that grooming brings and appreciate the joy of having a well-groomed and content Bullmastiff by your side.

Dental Care Basics

Taking care of your Bullmastiff's dental health is vital to their overall well-being. Just like humans, dogs can develop dental issues that can cause discomfort and impact their quality of life. By implementing proper dental care practices, you can help ensure that your Bullmastiff maintains strong teeth, healthy gums, and fresh breath. In this section, we'll explore the basics of dental care for your Bullmastiff and provide you with helpful tips to keep their pearly whites in tip-top shape.

Regular brushing is the cornerstone of dental care for your Bullmastiff. It's best to start this routine when they are young, but even if your Bullmastiff is older, it's never too late to introduce tooth brushing. Here are the steps to follow for effective tooth brushing:

1. Choose a dog-specific toothbrush and toothpaste. Human toothpaste can be harmful to dogs, so it's essential to use toothpaste specifically formulated for canines. The toothbrush should have soft bristles and be the appropriate size for your Bullmastiff's mouth.
2. Familiarize your Bullmastiff with the taste and texture of the toothpaste. Let them lick a small amount of toothpaste from your finger or the toothbrush. This helps them associate the taste with a positive experience.

3. Gently lift your Bullmastiff's lips and begin brushing the outer surfaces of their teeth using small, circular motions. Focus on the gum line and areas where plaque tends to accumulate.

4. Gradually increase the duration of the brushing sessions over time. Aim for brushing their teeth for two to three minutes, two to three times per week. Remember to be patient and give them breaks if needed.

5. Reward your Bullmastiff with praise, treats, or extra playtime after each successful brushing session. Positive reinforcement helps create a positive association with tooth brushing and makes it a more enjoyable experience for both of you.

Alongside regular tooth brushing, there are other ways to promote good dental health for your Bullmastiff. Dental chews and toys can help keep their teeth clean and reduce plaque buildup. Look for products that are specifically designed to promote chewing and help remove plaque. It's important to choose the right size chew or toy to prevent any choking hazards.

Regular veterinary check-ups are essential for your Bullmastiff's dental health. Your veterinarian can perform professional dental cleanings and check for any underlying dental issues. They can also provide guidance on home dental care and recommend appropriate dental treatments if needed. These check-ups allow for early detection of any dental problems and ensure that your Bullmastiff's oral health is closely monitored.

In addition to regular dental care, maintaining a healthy diet contributes to your Bullmastiff's dental well-being. Feeding them high-quality dog food that supports dental health can make a difference. Consult your veterinarian for recommendations on the best diet for your Bullmastiff's specific needs.

It's important to be vigilant and watch for any signs of dental problems in your Bullmastiff. Red or swollen gums, bad breath, excessive drooling, difficulty eating, or loose teeth are indications that dental issues may be present. If you notice any of these signs, it's crucial to consult your veterinarian for a thorough examination and appropriate treatment.

By prioritizing dental care in your grooming routine, you can help maintain your Bullmastiff's oral health and prevent dental problems. A healthy mouth leads to better overall health and a happier, more comfortable Bullmastiff. So, start brushing those teeth, explore dental chews and toys, and schedule regular veterinary check-ups to keep your Bullmastiff's smile shining bright.

Nail Trimming

Nail trimming is an essential aspect of grooming your Bullmastiff. Keeping their nails at an appropriate length is not only important for their comfort but also for their overall health and well-being.

Overgrown nails can cause discomfort, affect their gait, and even lead to potential injuries. In this section, we'll discuss the importance of nail trimming, share tips for successful trimming sessions, and guide you on how to keep your Bullmastiff's nails in great shape.

Regular nail trimming is necessary to maintain the proper length of your Bullmastiff's nails. Depending on their activity level and the surfaces they walk on, their nails may naturally wear down to some extent. However, regular trimming is still required to prevent overgrowth and potential issues. A good rule of thumb is to trim your Bullmastiff's nails every four to six weeks, but individual variation may require more frequent or less frequent trims.

To trim your Bullmastiff's nails, you'll need a pair of dog-specific nail clippers or a grinder. It's important to choose the right tool for your comfort and your Bullmastiff's nails. If you're unsure about which tool to use or how to trim their nails safely, consult a professional groomer or your veterinarian for guidance.

Before starting the trimming process, ensure that you and your Bullmastiff are in a calm and relaxed environment. Make sure you have proper lighting to see the nails clearly and avoid any distractions that may startle or agitate your Bullmastiff. If your Bullmastiff is new to nail trimming, introduce them to the clippers or grinder gradually. Let them sniff and inspect the tools so that they become familiar with them.

When you're ready to trim their nails, gently hold your Bullmastiff's paw in your hand. Be cautious not to squeeze or apply excessive pressure. Use your other hand to grasp their nail and extend it slightly. Identify the quick, which is the sensitive part of the nail that contains blood vessels and nerves. It's essential to avoid cutting into the quick, as it can cause bleeding and discomfort.

If your Bullmastiff has clear or light-colored nails, you can visually see the pinkish area within the nail called the quick. In this case, trim just below the quick, leaving a small margin to prevent accidentally cutting into it. If your Bullmastiff has dark-colored nails, it may be more challenging to identify the quick. In such cases, trim a small portion of the nail at a time, gradually working your way towards the desired length. As you trim, observe the center of the nail.

When you start to see a black dot or small dark circle, it's an indication that you're nearing the quick. If you accidentally trim into the quick and it starts bleeding, don't panic. Apply styptic powder or a styptic pencil to the nail to help stop the bleeding.

These products are available at pet supply stores and can be a valuable addition to your grooming kit. If you don't have styptic powder on hand, you can use cornstarch as a temporary solution. Apply gentle pressure to the bleeding nail using a clean cloth or tissue until the bleeding stops.

It's important to associate nail trimming with positive experiences for your Bullmastiff. Offer them treats, praise, and reassurance throughout the trimming process. This positive reinforcement helps create a positive association and makes future nail trims easier. If you're uncertain about trimming your Bullmastiff's nails or your Bullmastiff is particularly anxious or resistant to the process, consider seeking professional help from a groomer or veterinarian. They have the experience and expertise to trim nails safely and effectively.

In addition to regular nail trims, provide your Bullmastiff with opportunities to naturally wear down their nails. Regular exercise, especially on hard surfaces like concrete or asphalt, can help naturally file their nails. Just be cautious not to overexert your Bullmastiff or subject them to excessive pounding on hard surfaces.

By maintaining regular nail trimming as part of your grooming routine, you'll ensure that your Bullmastiff's nails are at a comfortable length. Trimming their nails not only promotes their comfort but also prevents potential injuries caused by overgrown nails. With patience, practice, and positive reinforcement, nail trimming can become a stress-free and rewarding experience for both you and your Bullmastiff.

Cleaning the Ears

Proper ear care is an essential part of grooming your Bullmastiff. Regular cleaning helps prevent ear infections, removes excess wax and debris, and ensures the overall health and comfort of your furry friend. In this section, we'll discuss the importance of cleaning your Bullmastiff's ears, provide guidance on how to clean them safely and effectively, and share tips to keep their ears in top condition.

Bullmastiffs have floppy ears that can be prone to moisture buildup, wax accumulation, and the growth of bacteria or yeast. It's important to establish a routine of cleaning their ears to keep them clean and healthy. The frequency of ear cleaning will vary depending on your Bullmastiff's individual needs, but typically once a month is sufficient for most dogs.

However, if your Bullmastiff is prone to ear infections or has excessive wax production, more frequent cleaning may be necessary.
To clean your Bullmastiff's ears, start by gathering the necessary supplies. You'll need a quality ear cleaning solution specifically formulated for dogs, cotton balls or gauze pads, and treats as a reward for your Bullmastiff's cooperation. Avoid using cotton swabs or any sharp objects inside the ear canal, as they can cause injury.

Choose a calm and quiet environment for the ear cleaning process. This helps minimize distractions and makes it easier for your Bullmastiff to remain relaxed. Begin by gently holding their ear flap and inspecting the outer part of the ear for any redness, swelling, or discharge. If you notice any abnormalities or signs of infection, such as a foul odor or excessive itching, it's best to consult your veterinarian for a thorough examination.

Next, apply a few drops of the ear cleaning solution into your Bullmastiff's ear canal. Gently massage the base of the ear for a few seconds to allow the solution to penetrate and loosen any debris or wax. This also helps your Bullmastiff become accustomed to the sensation and associate it with a positive experience.

Take a cotton ball or gauze pad and gently wipe the visible parts of the ear, including the ear flap and the entrance of the ear canal. Avoid inserting anything deep into the ear canal, as this can damage the delicate structures inside. Use a fresh cotton ball or gauze pad for each ear to prevent cross-contamination.

If you notice significant wax or debris inside the ear canal, you can use a cotton ball wrapped around your finger to gently clean the area. Be extremely gentle and do not force anything into the ear canal. If your Bullmastiff's ears are particularly dirty or they have a history of ear infections, it's recommended to consult your veterinarian for guidance on more extensive cleaning or treatment.

Remember to reward your Bullmastiff with treats and praise throughout the process. Positive reinforcement helps create a positive association with ear cleaning and makes future sessions more enjoyable for both of you.

In addition to regular cleaning, there are other measures you can take to promote good ear health for your Bullmastiff. Check their ears regularly for any signs of irritation, redness, swelling, or discharge. Keep their ears dry, especially after bathing or swimming, by gently drying them with a clean towel or using a pet-safe ear drying solution. Be mindful of allergens or irritants that may cause ear problems and take appropriate measures to minimize exposure.

It's important to note that if you notice any persistent or severe ear issues, it's best to consult your veterinarian for a thorough examination. They can determine the underlying cause of the problem and provide appropriate treatment.

By incorporating regular ear cleaning into your grooming routine and being attentive to any changes or issues, you'll help maintain your Bullmastiff's ear health and prevent potential ear infections. With patience, gentleness, and positive reinforcement, cleaning your Bullmastiff's ears can be a stress-free and beneficial experience for both of you.

Routine Health Checks at Home

Regular health checks at home are an essential part of grooming your Bullmastiff. By keeping a close eye on your dog's overall well-being, you can detect any potential health issues early and ensure they receive the necessary care. In this section, we'll discuss the importance of routine health checks, provide guidance on what to look for during these checks, and share tips to keep your Bullmastiff in optimal health.

Performing routine health checks at home allows you to monitor your Bullmastiff's physical condition and catch any changes or abnormalities. It's important to establish a consistent schedule for these checks, ideally once a month, to ensure that you don't miss any potential issues. Although your Bullmastiff may not always enjoy being examined, patience and positive reinforcement will help make these checks more manageable for both of you.

During a routine health check, start by examining your Bullmastiff's body from head to tail. Look for any visible signs of discomfort, such as limping, difficulty moving, or favoring certain areas. Check their coat for any changes in texture, excessive shedding, or skin issues like redness, rashes, or sores. Pay attention to their eyes, ensuring they are clear, bright, and free from discharge. Likewise, check their ears for any signs of redness, swelling, or discharge, which may indicate an ear infection. If you notice anything out of the ordinary, consult your veterinarian for further evaluation.

Next, examine your Bullmastiff's mouth and teeth. Look for any dental issues, such as plaque buildup, tartar, or redness and inflammation of the gums. Bad breath can also be an indicator of dental problems or other underlying issues. If you observe anything concerning, consult your veterinarian for a dental examination and appropriate treatment.

Check your Bullmastiff's paws for any cuts, sores, or foreign objects that may be lodged between their toes. Also, inspect their nails and trim them if necessary, following the guidelines we discussed in a previous section. Examine their pads for any signs of injury, cracking, or irritation.

While you're conducting the health check, pay attention to your Bullmastiff's behavior and energy level. Monitor their appetite, water intake, and bathroom habits to ensure they are consistent and normal. Any sudden changes in these areas may indicate an underlying health issue.

It's important to keep track of your Bullmastiff's weight and body condition. Regularly weigh your dog and observe their body shape. Obesity can lead to various health problems, so maintaining a healthy weight is crucial. If you have concerns about your Bullmastiff's weight, consult your veterinarian for guidance on proper nutrition and exercise.

During the health check, also inspect your Bullmastiff for external parasites, such as fleas or ticks. Check their fur thoroughly, paying attention to warm areas like armpits, groin, and ears. If you find any parasites, follow appropriate measures to remove them and prevent further infestation.

Routine health checks at home provide an opportunity for you to bond with your Bullmastiff and demonstrate your care and attentiveness. These checks allow you to catch any potential health issues early, which can lead to more effective treatment and better outcomes. Regular communication with your veterinarian is essential, and if you notice any significant changes or concerns during your health checks, don't hesitate to reach out to them for professional advice.

Remember, your Bullmastiff's health and well-being are of utmost importance. By performing routine health checks at home, you are taking an active role in their care and ensuring they live a happy and healthy life by your side.

Addressing Common Grooming Issues

As a Bullmastiff owner, you may come across various grooming issues that require your attention and care. Skin conditions, shedding, and other concerns can impact your Bullmastiff's comfort and overall well-being. In this section, we'll explore common grooming issues, discuss how to address them, and provide tips to keep your Bullmastiff looking and feeling their best.

Skin conditions are relatively common in Bullmastiffs and can manifest in different ways. Allergies, hot spots, dry skin, or irritations may occur, causing discomfort and itchiness for your furry friend. It's important to address these issues promptly to alleviate any discomfort and prevent further complications.

Regular grooming practices can help maintain healthy skin. Brush your Bullmastiff's coat regularly to remove loose fur, dirt, and debris. This not only keeps their coat looking neat but also helps distribute natural oils and stimulates blood circulation to the skin.

If your Bullmastiff experiences dry or flaky skin, consider adding a supplement rich in omega-3 fatty acids to their diet. Omega-3 fatty acids can help promote healthy skin and a shiny coat. Consult your veterinarian for recommendations on suitable supplements for your Bullmastiff.

If your Bullmastiff develops hot spots, which are areas of red, inflamed, and irritated skin, it's crucial to address them promptly. Keep the affected area clean by gently washing it with a mild, pet-safe shampoo. Applying a veterinarian-recommended antiseptic or topical treatment can help soothe the hot spot and promote healing. However, it's essential to consult your veterinarian for a proper diagnosis and treatment plan, as hot spots may have an underlying cause that needs to be addressed.

Shedding is another common grooming concern for Bullmastiffs. While they have a short and dense coat, they do shed moderately throughout the year. Regular brushing helps to remove loose hair and reduce shedding. Invest in a quality grooming tool, such as a deshedding brush or grooming glove, to effectively remove loose fur from your Bullmastiff's coat. During shedding seasons, which typically occur in spring and fall, your Bullmastiff may experience heavier shedding. Increase the frequency of brushing during these times to keep loose hair under control. It's also a good idea to groom your Bullmastiff outdoors or in an easily cleanable area to minimize the mess.

Bathing your Bullmastiff is an important part of their grooming routine, but it's essential to strike a balance. Excessive bathing can strip their skin of natural oils, leading to dryness and potential skin issues. Aim to bathe your Bullmastiff every few months or as needed, using a mild, dog-specific shampoo that won't irritate their skin. Consult your veterinarian for specific bathing recommendations based on your Bullmastiff's needs.

When addressing grooming issues, it's important to remember that each Bullmastiff is unique, and what works for one may not work for another. If you encounter persistent or severe grooming issues, it's best to consult your veterinarian. They can provide a proper diagnosis and recommend specific treatments or solutions tailored to your Bullmastiff's needs.

Regular grooming not only helps keep your Bullmastiff looking their best but also plays a crucial role in their overall health and comfort. By addressing common grooming issues promptly, you can ensure that your Bullmastiff stays happy, healthy, and free from discomfort. So, be attentive to their skin, manage shedding, and provide the necessary care to maintain their well-being and keep them feeling their best.

CHAPTER 9: BREEDING AND GENETICS

Breeding Bullmastiffs is a responsible and important endeavor that requires careful consideration and knowledge. In this chapter, we will explore the world of breeding and genetics, discussing key aspects such as the importance of understanding Bullmastiff genetics, ethical breeding practices, common genetically inherited health issues, the process of pregnancy and birth in Bullmastiffs, finding a reputable breeder, and determining if breeding Bullmastiffs is the right choice for you.

Understanding Bullmastiff genetics is crucial when it comes to breeding. It involves knowledge of hereditary traits, genetic diseases, and the principles of inheritance.

Breeding without a solid understanding of genetics can result in the propagation of health issues and undesirable traits. Therefore, it's important to educate yourself about the breed's genetic makeup and work with knowledgeable breeders or veterinarians who can provide guidance.

Ethical breeding practices are paramount to maintaining the health and well-being of the Bullmastiff breed. Responsible breeders prioritize the health and temperament of the dogs they breed, carefully selecting mating pairs to improve the overall quality of the breed. They conduct health screenings, such as hip and elbow evaluations, cardiac exams, and genetic testing, to ensure that the parent dogs are free from hereditary health issues. Ethical breeders also adhere to breed standards set by reputable kennel clubs and organizations.

Common genetically inherited health issues can occur in Bullmastiffs, and it's important for breeders to be aware of these conditions and take steps to minimize their occurrence. Conditions such as hip and elbow dysplasia, progressive retinal atrophy, and heart disease are among the genetic health concerns that can be found in the breed. By conducting proper health screenings and selecting breeding pairs with healthy genetic backgrounds, breeders can help reduce the risk of passing on these inherited conditions to future generations.

The process of pregnancy and birth in Bullmastiffs requires careful monitoring and support. During pregnancy, the dam should receive appropriate nutrition and veterinary care to ensure the health of both the mother and the developing puppies. As the due date approaches, it's important to create a comfortable and safe whelping area for the dam to give birth. Breeders should be prepared for potential complications during labor and have a plan in place to provide necessary assistance if needed. Proper socialization and care for the puppies after birth are also crucial for their healthy development.

When considering breeding Bullmastiffs, finding a reputable breeder is essential. Reputable breeders prioritize the health and well-being of their dogs and are committed to preserving the breed's integrity. They conduct proper health screenings, provide appropriate socialization and care for their puppies, and offer ongoing support and guidance to puppy buyers. Researching and connecting with reputable breeders can ensure that you are working with individuals who have the breed's best interests at heart.

Breeding Bullmastiffs is a significant responsibility that requires time, effort, and financial resources. It's important to evaluate your own capabilities and commitment before deciding to become a breeder. Breeding should never be undertaken for financial gain alone but rather with the intention of preserving and improving the breed. Responsible breeders prioritize the welfare of their dogs and the betterment of the breed as a whole.

In conclusion, breeding Bullmastiffs is a complex and important undertaking. Understanding Bullmastiff genetics, practicing ethical breeding, being aware of common genetically inherited health issues, and providing proper care during pregnancy and birth are all crucial elements of responsible breeding. By working with reputable breeders and evaluating your own capabilities and commitment, you can contribute to the preservation and improvement of this wonderful breed while ensuring the health and well-being of Bullmastiffs for generations to come.

An Introduction to Bullmastiff Genetics

Understanding Bullmastiff genetics is fundamental to responsible breeding practices and the overall health and well-being of the breed. In this section, we will delve into the world of Bullmastiff genetics, exploring key concepts such as hereditary traits, genetic diseases, and the principles of inheritance.

Genetics plays a vital role in shaping the characteristics and traits of Bullmastiffs. Every Bullmastiff inherits genetic material from its parents, which determines its physical appearance, temperament, and potential health issues. By understanding these genetic principles, breeders can make informed decisions when it comes to selecting mating pairs and improving the breed.

One important concept in Bullmastiff genetics is the inheritance of traits. Some traits are controlled by a single gene, while others are influenced by multiple genes. For example, coat color is determined by several genes, while certain health conditions may be controlled by a single gene mutation. By studying the inheritance patterns of specific traits, breeders can predict the likelihood of passing them on to future generations.

Genetic diseases are another significant aspect of Bullmastiff genetics. Like any other breed, Bullmastiffs can be susceptible to certain genetic conditions. It is crucial for breeders to be aware of these diseases and take necessary steps to minimize their occurrence.

Common genetic health issues in Bullmastiffs include hip and elbow dysplasia, progressive retinal atrophy, and heart disease. By conducting health screenings and genetic tests, breeders can make informed decisions to avoid breeding dogs that carry these genetic diseases.

The principles of inheritance, such as dominance and recessiveness, are fundamental in understanding how traits are passed on from one generation to the next. Dominant traits are expressed even when present in only one copy of the gene, while recessive traits require two copies of the gene for expression. This knowledge helps breeders determine the likelihood of certain traits or genetic conditions appearing in future litters.

To further enhance their understanding of Bullmastiff genetics, breeders can utilize tools such as pedigrees and DNA testing. Pedigrees provide a visual representation of a dog's lineage, allowing breeders to trace the presence of specific traits or genetic conditions in past generations. DNA testing can provide valuable information about a dog's genetic makeup and help identify carriers of specific genetic diseases.

Breeders who have a solid grasp of Bullmastiff genetics can make informed decisions when selecting mating pairs. They aim to breed dogs that complement each other genetically, with the goal of producing offspring that possess desirable traits and are free from known genetic diseases. Through careful selection and responsible breeding practices, breeders can contribute to the overall health and preservation of the Bullmastiff breed.

In conclusion, Bullmastiff genetics is a fascinating and vital aspect of responsible breeding. Understanding hereditary traits, genetic diseases, and the principles of inheritance empowers breeders to make informed decisions when selecting mating pairs. By prioritizing the health and well-being of the breed and utilizing tools such as pedigrees and DNA testing, breeders can contribute to the preservation and improvement of the Bullmastiff breed for future generations to enjoy.

Steps and Considerations in Breeding Bullmastiffs

Breeding Bullmastiffs is a significant undertaking that requires careful planning, preparation, and consideration. In this section, we will explore the steps and considerations involved in breeding Bullmastiffs, ensuring the health and well-being of the dogs and the preservation of the breed.

The first step in breeding Bullmastiffs is to thoroughly research and understand the breed. Familiarize yourself with the breed standards, temperament traits, and any specific health concerns that may be prevalent in Bullmastiffs. Educate yourself on the principles of genetics and inheritance, as this knowledge will help you make informed decisions throughout the breeding process.

Selecting suitable breeding pairs is a crucial consideration in Bullmastiff breeding. Look for dogs that complement each other in terms of temperament, physical conformation, and overall health. The goal is to produce offspring that embody the best qualities of the breed. Consult with experienced breeders, attend dog shows, and seek guidance from breed clubs to identify potential mating pairs that align with your breeding goals.

Before proceeding with the breeding, ensure that both the male and female dogs are in optimal health. Schedule a pre-breeding examination with a veterinarian to evaluate their overall health, conduct necessary health screenings, and ensure they are free from any genetic diseases or conditions that could be passed on to the offspring. It's important to prioritize the well-being of the dogs and avoid breeding individuals with significant health issues.

Timing is critical when it comes to breeding Bullmastiffs. Monitor the female dog's estrus cycle to determine the optimal time for mating. This typically involves observing physical and behavioral changes, such as swelling of the vulva and changes in behavior. Consult with your veterinarian for guidance on timing and to determine the most fertile period for successful breeding.

Once the female dog is determined to be in the appropriate stage of her estrus cycle, introduce her to the chosen male dog in a controlled and supervised environment. Allow them to interact naturally while closely monitoring their behavior. It's important to ensure a safe and stress-free environment during the mating process.

After successful mating, continue to provide proper care and support to the pregnant female. Ensure she receives a balanced diet, regular exercise, and veterinary check-ups throughout her pregnancy. Monitor her closely for any signs of complications or discomfort, and be prepared for the possibility of requiring veterinary assistance during the birthing process.

As responsible breeders, it's important to have a plan in place for the care and socialization of the puppies once they are born. Provide a clean and comfortable whelping area for the dam and her puppies. Ensure they have access to appropriate nutrition, warmth, and early socialization experiences. Regular veterinary check-ups for the puppies are essential to monitor their growth and overall health.

Throughout the breeding process, maintain open communication and build relationships with the puppy buyers. Screen potential buyers carefully, ensuring they understand the responsibilities of Bullmastiff ownership and have the means to provide a loving and suitable home for the puppies. Offer ongoing support and guidance to the new owners, fostering a positive relationship and ensuring the well-being of the puppies beyond their initial departure.

Breeding Bullmastiffs is a journey that requires dedication, knowledge, and a deep love for the breed. By following these steps and considerations, you can contribute to the preservation and improvement of the Bullmastiff breed while ensuring the health and well-being of the dogs involved. Remember, responsible breeding is a lifelong commitment, and your efforts will have a lasting impact on the future of this wonderful breed.

Ethical Breeding Practices

Ethical breeding practices are the foundation of responsible Bullmastiff breeding. By adhering to these practices, breeders prioritize the health, temperament, and well-being of the dogs involved while working towards the preservation and improvement of the Bullmastiff breed. In this section, we will explore the key aspects of ethical breeding practices that should guide breeders in their journey.

One of the fundamental principles of ethical breeding is selecting mating pairs that complement each other in terms of temperament, physical conformation, and overall health. The goal is to produce offspring that embody the best qualities of the breed while minimizing the risk of passing on genetic diseases or undesirable traits. This requires careful consideration and research to find suitable breeding partners that will contribute positively to the breed.

Health screening is a crucial aspect of ethical breeding. Before breeding, both the male and female dogs should undergo comprehensive health evaluations, including hip and elbow evaluations, cardiac exams, and genetic testing for known genetic diseases. These screenings help ensure that the breeding dogs are free from significant health issues that could be passed on to their offspring. By prioritizing the health of the dogs, breeders contribute to the overall well-being and longevity of the breed.

Maintaining accurate records and pedigrees is another important component of ethical breeding. By keeping meticulous records of the lineage and health information of the dogs involved, breeders can make informed decisions about breeding pairs and track the presence of specific traits or genetic conditions in future generations. Accurate pedigrees also provide transparency to puppy buyers, allowing them to understand the lineage and potential health risks associated with their chosen puppy.

Responsible breeders prioritize the well-being and proper socialization of their dogs and puppies. They provide a safe and clean environment for the dogs, ensuring access to appropriate nutrition, exercise, and veterinary care. Puppies are given early socialization experiences to help them develop into well-rounded individuals. Ethical breeders go above and beyond to ensure that their puppies are placed in loving and suitable homes, carefully screening potential buyers and providing ongoing support and guidance throughout the life of the dog.

Ethical breeders also participate in breed clubs and organizations, staying informed about the latest developments in the breed and actively engaging with the Bullmastiff community. They strive to contribute positively to the breed through their involvement in events such as dog shows, competitions, and breed-specific activities. By actively participating in the breed community, breeders have the opportunity to learn from others, share knowledge and experiences, and continuously improve their breeding practices.

Transparency and honesty are paramount in ethical breeding. Breeders provide full disclosure of any known health issues, genetic test results, and the potential risks associated with the breed. They are open and accessible to answer questions from potential puppy buyers and provide accurate and honest information about the breed's characteristics, requirements, and potential challenges. By fostering trust and open communication, ethical breeders build strong relationships with their puppy buyers and the Bullmastiff community at large.

In conclusion, ethical breeding practices are crucial for the health, well-being, and preservation of the Bullmastiff breed. By selecting suitable breeding pairs, conducting thorough health screenings, maintaining accurate records, prioritizing the well-being of the dogs and puppies, and actively engaging in the breed community, ethical breeders contribute to the ongoing improvement of the breed while ensuring that future generations of Bullmastiffs thrive in loving and responsible homes.

Common Genetically Inherited Health Issues

As a responsible Bullmastiff breeder, it is essential to be aware of the common genetically inherited health issues that can affect the breed. By understanding these conditions, breeders can make informed decisions to minimize their occurrence and prioritize the overall health and well-being of the dogs they breed. In this section, we will explore some of the most prevalent genetically inherited health issues in Bullmastiffs.

Hip and elbow dysplasia are among the most common genetic health concerns in Bullmastiffs. These conditions involve abnormal development of the hip and elbow joints, leading to varying degrees of pain, lameness, and joint deterioration. Breeding dogs should undergo hip and elbow evaluations conducted by certified veterinary specialists to assess their joint health. By selecting breeding pairs with good hip and elbow scores, breeders can help reduce the risk of these conditions in their offspring.

Progressive retinal atrophy (PRA) is another genetically inherited condition that affects Bullmastiffs. PRA is a group of degenerative eye diseases that lead to progressive vision loss and, in severe cases, blindness. DNA testing can identify carriers of the PRA gene, allowing breeders to make informed decisions about mating pairs and avoid producing offspring affected by this condition. Responsible breeders prioritize breeding dogs that are free from the PRA gene mutation to minimize the risk of passing it on to future generations.

Heart disease, such as dilated cardiomyopathy (DCM), is a concern in the Bullmastiff breed. DCM is a condition that affects the heart muscle, leading to enlargement and reduced cardiac function. Regular cardiac evaluations, including echocardiograms and electrocardiograms, can help identify dogs with signs of heart disease. Breeding dogs with a clean bill of cardiac health and no history of heart disease can help minimize the risk of passing on these conditions to their offspring.

Another genetic health issue that can affect Bullmastiffs is hypothyroidism. Hypothyroidism occurs when the thyroid gland fails to produce sufficient amounts of thyroid hormones, leading to various health problems, including weight gain, lethargy, and skin issues. Thyroid function tests can help identify dogs with hypothyroidism. Breeding dogs should be screened for thyroid disorders to reduce the risk of passing on this condition.

Responsible breeders prioritize the health of their dogs by conducting thorough health screenings and genetic tests. By selecting breeding pairs that are free from known genetic diseases and have a clean bill of health, breeders can help reduce the incidence of these conditions in future generations. It is essential to stay informed about the latest research and advancements in genetic testing to make the most informed breeding decisions.

In addition to genetic testing, maintaining accurate health records and pedigrees is crucial. Keeping detailed records allows breeders to track the presence of specific health issues in their breeding lines and make informed decisions about potential mating pairs. Accurate pedigrees also provide transparency to puppy buyers, enabling them to make informed decisions about their chosen puppy and understand any potential health risks associated with the breed.

Educating puppy buyers about these common genetically inherited health issues is also important. Providing information on the importance of health screenings, genetic testing, and responsible breeding practices empowers puppy buyers to make informed decisions and ensures that they are prepared to provide the necessary care for their Bullmastiffs throughout their lives.

By understanding and addressing the common genetically inherited health issues in Bullmastiffs, responsible breeders play a vital role in preserving the health and well-being of the breed. Through careful selection of breeding pairs, thorough health screenings, and transparent communication with puppy buyers, breeders can contribute to the production of healthy Bullmastiffs with a reduced risk of inheriting genetic health conditions.

The Process of Pregnancy and Birth in Bullmastiffs

The journey of bringing new life into the world is an exciting and rewarding experience for Bullmastiff breeders. Understanding the process of pregnancy and birth is crucial to ensuring the health and well-being of both the dam and the puppies. In this section, we will explore the stages of pregnancy, the signs of impending birth, and the care needed during this special time.

The pregnancy of a Bullmastiff typically lasts around 63 days, although it can vary slightly from dog to dog. During the first few weeks, it may be challenging to detect signs of pregnancy, but as the weeks progress, you may notice some changes in the dam's behavior and physical appearance. She may experience increased appetite, weight gain, and changes in nipple size and color.

Around the fourth week of pregnancy, a veterinarian can confirm the pregnancy through methods such as ultrasound or palpation. This confirmation allows you to start preparing for the upcoming birth and ensure that the dam receives the necessary care.
As the pregnancy continues, it is essential to provide the dam with a balanced diet to support her nutritional needs. Consult with your veterinarian to determine the appropriate diet and portion sizes for the pregnant dam. It's crucial to avoid overfeeding, as excessive weight gain can lead to complications during birth.

During the final weeks of pregnancy, you may notice behavioral changes in the dam. She may seek out a quiet and comfortable space to prepare for birth, known as nesting behavior. It's important to provide her with a clean and cozy whelping area where she can feel safe and secure.

Signs of impending birth, also known as whelping, include restlessness, loss of appetite, nesting behavior, and a drop in body temperature. The dam's body temperature may decrease by around 1 to 2 degrees Fahrenheit, signaling that labor is approaching. It's a good idea to keep a close eye on her and be prepared for the birth process.

During labor, the dam will experience contractions as she gives birth to her puppies. It's essential to allow her to progress through labor naturally without interference unless there are indications of complications. Be present to offer support and assistance if needed, but let the dam take the lead. Each puppy is usually born within 30 to 60 minutes of the previous one, although there can be variations.

After the birth of each puppy, the dam will instinctively clean and care for her newborns by licking them to stimulate their breathing and remove the birth sac. Observe closely to ensure that each puppy is breathing and nursing properly. If there are any concerns about a puppy's health or if the dam is unable to care for them adequately, consult with a veterinarian for guidance.

In the days following the birth, provide a warm and comfortable environment for the dam and her puppies. Monitor their weight gain and ensure that each puppy is receiving sufficient nourishment from nursing. If necessary, consult with your veterinarian about supplementing the dam's milk or introducing puppy formula to support the puppies' growth.
As the puppies grow, continue to provide proper care, including regular veterinary check-ups, vaccinations, and early socialization experiences. Monitor their development and assist with the weaning process when the time is right.

The process of pregnancy and birth in Bullmastiffs is a special and delicate time. By understanding the stages of pregnancy, being vigilant for signs of impending birth, and providing the necessary care, you can help ensure the health and well-being of both the dam and her precious puppies. Remember to seek guidance from your veterinarian throughout the process to address any concerns and ensure a smooth and successful birthing experience.

Finding a Reputable Breeder

Finding a reputable breeder is crucial when considering adding a Bullmastiff to your family. A reputable breeder not only ensures the health and well-being of the dogs they breed but also provides ongoing support and guidance to puppy buyers. In this section, we will explore the key factors to consider when searching for a reputable Bullmastiff breeder.

One of the first steps in finding a reputable breeder is to conduct thorough research. Start by seeking recommendations from trusted sources, such as local breed clubs, veterinarians, or Bullmastiff enthusiasts. Online platforms and breed-specific forums can also be valuable resources for connecting with reputable breeders. Take the time to read reviews, testimonials, and gather as much information as possible about potential breeders.

When evaluating breeders, it's important to consider their experience and knowledge of the Bullmastiff breed. Reputable breeders will have a deep understanding of the breed's history, temperament, and potential health issues. They should be able to provide detailed information about their breeding program, including health screenings, genetic testing, and the steps they take to produce healthy and well-socialized puppies.

Visiting the breeder's facilities is highly recommended to assess the living conditions of the dogs. A reputable breeder will maintain a clean and safe environment for their dogs, providing adequate space, proper nutrition, and regular veterinary care. Observe the behavior of the dogs and ensure that they are well-socialized and interact positively with people.

A reputable breeder will be transparent about the health history of their breeding dogs and their puppies. They will provide health clearances for genetic diseases and share information about any potential health concerns in their breeding lines. Ask for documentation of health screenings and inquire about the steps taken to ensure the overall health of the puppies.

An important aspect of finding a reputable breeder is their commitment to responsible breeding practices. They will have a clear breeding plan and goals in mind, focusing on improving the breed and producing puppies that adhere to breed standards.

They will have a limited number of litters per year to ensure proper care and attention to each puppy. Reputable breeders prioritize the well-being and proper socialization of their puppies. They will provide early socialization experiences, exposing the puppies to various stimuli, environments, and experiences to help them develop into well-rounded individuals. They will also offer guidance and support to new puppy owners, assisting with the transition and providing ongoing advice as the puppy grows.

When communicating with a breeder, ask questions about their breeding program, their involvement in the Bullmastiff community, and their policies regarding health guarantees, contracts, and return policies. A reputable breeder will be open and willing to answer your questions, addressing any concerns you may have.

Attending dog shows and events is an excellent way to meet reputable breeders in person and see their dogs in action. It allows you to interact with the breeder, observe the temperament and quality of their dogs, and establish a personal connection.

Remember, reputable breeders prioritize the health and well-being of their dogs and are committed to the betterment of the breed. They invest time, effort, and resources into producing healthy and well-socialized puppies. By choosing a reputable breeder, you are not only bringing home a Bullmastiff but also gaining a lifelong resource and support system for your journey as a Bullmastiff owner.

Deciding if Breeding Bullmastiffs is Right for You

Breeding Bullmastiffs is a significant responsibility that requires careful consideration and commitment. It's essential to evaluate your motivations, resources, and the impact breeding will have on your life and the lives of the dogs involved. In this section, we will explore the factors to consider when deciding if breeding Bullmastiffs is the right path for you.

First and foremost, it's important to have a genuine passion for the Bullmastiff breed. Breeding should not be solely driven by financial gain but rather by a deep love and appreciation for the breed's characteristics, temperament, and history. Breeding Bullmastiffs is a long-term commitment, and your dedication should extend beyond the puppies' cute and cuddly stage.

Educate yourself about the breed's standard, health concerns, and breed-specific traits. Familiarize yourself with the responsibilities that come with breeding, including the health screenings, genetic testing, and ongoing care required. Being knowledgeable about the breed will help you make informed decisions and contribute to the betterment of the Bullmastiff breed.

Consider your resources and the time commitment required for breeding Bullmastiffs. Breeding involves investing time, effort, and financial resources into health screenings, genetic testing, proper nutrition, veterinary care, and providing a suitable environment for the dogs and puppies. It's essential to assess your ability to meet these requirements and provide the necessary care for the well-being of the dogs.

Evaluate your ability to prioritize the health and welfare of the breed. Responsible breeders prioritize the health and well-being of their dogs, which means making informed decisions about breeding pairs, conducting health screenings, and providing appropriate care for the dam and puppies. Breeding should not be taken lightly, as it directly impacts the future generations of Bullmastiffs.

Consider the potential emotional challenges associated with breeding. Breeding includes the joys of seeing new life and contributing to the breed but also the responsibility of caring for the dam during pregnancy and whelping, making difficult decisions about puppy placement, and dealing with potential health concerns. It's essential to be emotionally prepared for the highs and lows that come with breeding.

Evaluate your ability to provide ongoing support and guidance to puppy buyers. Responsible breeders establish long-lasting relationships with puppy buyers, offering advice, guidance, and support throughout the life of the puppy. This includes being a resource for training, health concerns, and addressing any challenges that arise. The commitment to supporting the puppy buyers extends far beyond the initial sale.

Consider your ability to handle the potential challenges of finding suitable homes for the puppies. Responsible breeders carefully screen potential puppy buyers to ensure they can provide a loving and suitable environment for a Bullmastiff. This process may involve turning away potential buyers who may not meet the necessary criteria. Finding the right homes for the puppies is essential for their well-being and future.

Breeding Bullmastiffs should not be undertaken lightly. It requires a deep understanding of the breed, a commitment to the well-being of the dogs, and a passion for preserving and improving the breed. Take the time to assess your motivations, resources, and capabilities before embarking on a breeding journey.

If breeding Bullmastiffs aligns with your values, knowledge, and commitment, it can be a rewarding and fulfilling experience. Responsible breeders play a vital role in the preservation and betterment of the breed, contributing to the future generations of healthy and well-tempered Bullmastiffs.

CHAPTER 10: BULLMASTIFFS AND LEGISLATION

Understanding and Navigating Breed-Specific Laws and Restrictions

Bullmastiffs, like many other dog breeds, are sometimes subject to breed-specific legislation and restrictions. These laws and regulations vary from one jurisdiction to another and can have a significant impact on Bullmastiff owners. In this section, we will explore the subject of breed-specific legislation, owner responsibilities according to the law, the influence of public perception, and how to protect yourself and your Bullmastiff legally.

Breed-specific legislation (BSL) refers to laws and regulations that target specific dog breeds based on perceived risks or negative stereotypes. These laws often impose restrictions on ownership, such as mandatory muzzling, leash requirements, licensing, insurance, and even outright bans. It's crucial for Bullmastiff owners to familiarize themselves with the specific laws and regulations in their local area.

When it comes to breed-specific legislation, it's essential to understand your responsibilities as a Bullmastiff owner.

Take the time to research and comprehend the specific requirements and restrictions outlined by your local authorities. This includes adhering to leash laws, licensing regulations, and any specific provisions related to Bullmastiffs. By being a responsible and law-abiding owner, you can help combat negative stereotypes associated with the breed.

Public perception plays a significant role in the development and enforcement of breed-specific legislation. It's unfortunate that certain dog breeds, including Bullmastiffs, have been unfairly stigmatized due to misconceptions and negative media portrayal.

As a Bullmastiff owner, you have the opportunity to challenge these misconceptions by being a responsible owner, promoting positive interactions with your dog, and educating others about the breed's true nature.

To protect yourself and your Bullmastiff legally, it's essential to be aware of your rights and the laws that pertain to dog ownership in your area. Familiarize yourself with local ordinances, licensing requirements, and liability laws. It's also crucial to obtain appropriate insurance coverage that complies with local regulations. By taking proactive steps to comply with the law, you can ensure the safety and well-being of your Bullmastiff and mitigate potential legal issues.

Advocacy is another crucial aspect when it comes to breed-specific legislation. Joining forces with local breed clubs, dog owner associations, and advocacy groups can strengthen your voice and influence policymakers. By engaging in constructive conversations, providing accurate information about Bullmastiffs, and advocating for responsible dog ownership, you can contribute to positive change and challenge breed-specific laws and restrictions.

In addition to breed-specific legislation, it's important to stay informed about general dog ownership laws and regulations. This includes responsible ownership practices, such as properly restraining and controlling your Bullmastiff in public, cleaning up after them, and ensuring their behavior does not pose a threat to others. By being a responsible owner, you can help shape a positive perception of Bullmastiffs and dog ownership in general.

Finally, seek legal advice if you encounter any legal issues or challenges related to your Bullmastiff. An attorney with experience in dog-related matters can provide guidance and support, ensuring that your rights and the rights of your Bullmastiff are protected.

While breed-specific legislation and restrictions can be frustrating and challenging for Bullmastiff owners, it's important to approach the issue with knowledge, responsibility, and a commitment to advocating for fair and reasonable laws. By being an informed and responsible owner, you can help challenge stereotypes, protect your Bullmastiff, and contribute to a positive and inclusive community for all dog owners.

Breed-Specific Laws and Restrictions

Breed-specific laws and restrictions are a topic of concern for Bullmastiff owners, as these regulations can have a direct impact on how they can care for and enjoy their beloved dogs. Breed-specific legislation refers to laws that target specific breeds based on perceived risks or negative stereotypes. While the intention behind these laws is often to promote public safety, it's essential to understand their implications and navigate them responsibly as a Bullmastiff owner.

Breed-specific laws can vary widely depending on the jurisdiction you live in. Some areas may impose restrictions or requirements for owning Bullmastiffs, such as mandatory muzzling in public, leash and licensing regulations, and special permits. In extreme cases, certain jurisdictions may even ban ownership of Bullmastiffs or other breeds entirely.

To ensure compliance with breed-specific laws, it's crucial to familiarize yourself with the specific regulations in your local area. Research and understand the ordinances and requirements that apply to Bullmastiffs, including any restrictions on public spaces, licensing, or liability insurance. By having a clear understanding of the laws, you can avoid unnecessary legal complications and ensure the safety of your Bullmastiff and the community.

While breed-specific laws can be frustrating and challenging, it's important to approach the issue with a responsible mindset. As a Bullmastiff owner, it's your responsibility to demonstrate the true nature and temperament of the breed through responsible ownership practices. By being a responsible owner, you can help challenge negative stereotypes and promote a positive image of Bullmastiffs in your community.

One way to mitigate the impact of breed-specific legislation is by promoting responsible dog ownership. Ensure that your Bullmastiff receives proper training and socialization, follows leash laws, and exhibits good behavior in public spaces. By being a responsible owner, you can help change public perception and showcase the well-mannered and gentle nature of Bullmastiffs.

Advocacy plays a crucial role in addressing breed-specific laws and restrictions. Get involved with local breed clubs, dog owner associations, and advocacy groups to voice your concerns and support changes to unfair legislation. Educate others about

Bullmastiffs, their temperament, and their positive contributions to society. By engaging in constructive conversations, you can help challenge misconceptions and promote fair and reasonable laws that focus on responsible ownership rather than breed discrimination.

It's important to remember that laws can change over time, and advocacy efforts can make a difference. Stay informed about proposed changes to breed-specific legislation in your area and actively participate in discussions and public hearings. Your voice matters, and by sharing your knowledge and experiences as a Bullmastiff owner, you can help shape a more inclusive and fair legal environment for all dog owners.

In conclusion, breed-specific laws and restrictions can present challenges for Bullmastiff owners, but by understanding the regulations in your area, being a responsible owner, and actively engaging in advocacy efforts, you can help protect your Bullmastiff's rights and work towards fair and inclusive legislation. By promoting responsible ownership and challenging stereotypes, you can showcase the true nature of Bullmastiffs and contribute to a more inclusive and understanding community for all dog lovers.

Owner Responsibilities According to Law

As a Bullmastiff owner, it's important to understand your responsibilities according to the law. Each jurisdiction may have specific requirements and regulations that govern dog ownership, and being aware of these responsibilities is essential to ensure the well-being of your Bullmastiff and maintain a positive relationship with your community. In this section, we will discuss some common owner responsibilities according to the law.

Licensing and registration: Many jurisdictions require dog owners to obtain a license or register their dogs with the local authorities. This helps ensure that dogs are properly identified and can be traced back to their owners. Check the regulations in your area and ensure that your Bullmastiff is licensed or registered as required. This typically involves providing proof of vaccinations and paying a fee.

Leash laws: Leash laws are designed to promote public safety and prevent dogs from running at large. It's important to adhere to leash laws in your area and keep your Bullmastiff on a leash when in public spaces. This not only helps maintain control over your dog but also demonstrates responsible ownership and consideration for others.

Poop-scooping: Cleaning up after your Bullmastiff is not only a matter of courtesy but also a legal requirement in many jurisdictions. Properly dispose of your dog's waste in designated receptacles or follow local regulations regarding waste disposal. This helps keep public areas clean and prevents the spread of disease.

Responsible control: It's your responsibility as a Bullmastiff owner to ensure that your dog is under control at all times. This means preventing your dog from causing harm or nuisance to others. Train your Bullmastiff to obey basic commands, such as "sit" and "stay," and practice good manners when interacting with people and other animals.

Proper confinement: Some jurisdictions have regulations regarding the proper confinement of dogs on your property. This may include requirements for secure fencing or the use of outdoor enclosures. Ensure that your Bullmastiff is safely contained within your property and cannot escape or pose a threat to others.

Public nuisance: As a responsible Bullmastiff owner, it's important to prevent your dog from becoming a public nuisance. Excessive barking, aggressive behavior, or any actions that disturb the peace and tranquility of your community may lead to complaints and legal repercussions. Take proactive steps to address any behavioral issues and ensure that your Bullmastiff is a well-behaved member of society.

Liability insurance: Some jurisdictions require dog owners, particularly those with certain breeds, to carry liability insurance. This provides financial protection in the event that your Bullmastiff causes injury or property damage to others. Check the regulations in your area to determine if liability insurance is required and obtain the appropriate coverage if necessary.

It's important to note that laws and regulations may vary depending on where you live, so it's essential to familiarize yourself with the specific requirements in your jurisdiction. Stay updated on any changes in the law and ensure that you comply with any new regulations that may be implemented.

By understanding and fulfilling your responsibilities as a Bullmastiff owner according to the law, you can contribute to a harmonious relationship between dog owners and the community. Responsible ownership not only ensures the safety and well-being of your Bullmastiff but also fosters positive perceptions of the breed and promotes a respectful and inclusive environment for all.

The Impact of Public Perception on Breed-Specific Legislation

Public perception plays a significant role in the development, enforcement, and impact of breed-specific legislation (BSL). The way people perceive certain dog breeds, including Bullmastiffs, can shape the laws and regulations that govern their ownership. In this section, we will explore the impact of public perception on breed-specific legislation and the importance of challenging stereotypes.

Public perception is often influenced by media portrayals and popular culture. Unfortunately, some dog breeds, including Bullmastiffs, have been subjected to negative stereotypes and misconceptions. These stereotypes can lead to an unfair and biased perception of the breed, contributing to the development of breed-specific legislation that targets specific breeds based on assumptions rather than actual behavior or evidence.

The negative portrayal of certain dog breeds in the media can lead to a climate of fear and misinformation. When incidents involving dogs occur, especially those that involve aggressive behavior or attacks, media coverage often focuses on breed identification, even if the dog involved is not accurately identified. This kind of sensationalism can perpetuate existing stereotypes and create an atmosphere of fear and misunderstanding around certain breeds.

Public perception can be influenced by personal experiences, anecdotes, and individual biases. If someone has had a negative encounter with a Bullmastiff or heard stories that reinforce negative stereotypes, it can shape their perception of the entire breed. Challenging these preconceived notions and educating the public about the true nature of

Bullmastiffs is crucial to combatting breed-specific legislation and promoting fair treatment of all dogs.

It's important to emphasize that a dog's behavior is primarily influenced by factors such as socialization, training, and individual temperament, rather than breed alone. Bullmastiffs, like any other breed, can be gentle, loving, and well-behaved when properly cared for and raised in a positive environment. It is unfair to judge an entire breed based on the actions of a few individuals.

By being responsible Bullmastiff owners and showcasing the breed's positive attributes, we can challenge negative perceptions. Proper training, socialization, and responsible ownership practices help demonstrate the true nature of Bullmastiffs and counteract stereotypes. Encouraging positive interactions between Bullmastiffs and the community, such as participating in therapy dog programs or engaging in public events, can also help change public perception.

Education is a powerful tool in shifting public perception. Providing accurate information about Bullmastiffs, their temperament, and their history can help dispel myths and misconceptions. Engaging in conversations with others, sharing personal experiences, and providing opportunities for people to meet well-behaved Bullmastiffs can help break down barriers and foster understanding.

By actively challenging stereotypes and engaging in constructive conversations, Bullmastiff owners can play a crucial role in influencing public perception and addressing breed-specific legislation. Collaborating with local breed clubs, dog owner associations, and advocacy groups can amplify your voice and create a united front in advocating for fair and evidence-based legislation.

It's important to remember that changing public perception is a long-term endeavor that requires patience, persistence, and a commitment to responsible ownership. By showcasing the true nature of Bullmastiffs and promoting responsible dog ownership practices, we can contribute to a society that values all dogs as individuals, regardless of breed, and works towards legislation that focuses on responsible ownership rather than discriminatory practices.

How to Protect Yourself and Your Bullmastiff Legally

As a Bullmastiff owner, it's important to take proactive steps to protect yourself and your beloved companion legally. Breed-specific legislation and other legal considerations can present challenges, but with the right knowledge and precautions, you can ensure the safety and well-being of your Bullmastiff while navigating the legal landscape. In this section, we will discuss some practical ways to protect yourself and your Bullmastiff legally.

1. Familiarize yourself with the laws: Stay informed about the laws and regulations that apply to dog ownership in your jurisdiction. This includes not only breed-specific legislation but also general dog ownership laws, licensing

requirements, leash laws, and any other relevant regulations. Knowledge of the law is your first line of defense in ensuring compliance and avoiding legal issues.

2. Obtain appropriate insurance coverage: Consider obtaining liability insurance that covers your Bullmastiff. This type of insurance provides financial protection in case your dog causes injury or property damage to others. Review your insurance policies to ensure they cover any potential breed-specific liabilities and fulfill any requirements set by your local authorities.

3. Maintain up-to-date licenses and vaccinations: Keep your Bullmastiff's licenses and vaccinations current as required by law. Regularly update your dog's licensing information and ensure that they receive necessary vaccinations and health checks. Compliance with these regulations not only demonstrates responsible ownership but also ensures the health and safety of your Bullmastiff and those around them.

4. Secure your property: Take measures to secure your property and prevent your Bullmastiff from escaping or posing a threat to others. This may involve installing secure fencing, ensuring gates are locked, and creating designated areas where your dog can safely enjoy outdoor time. By providing a safe and controlled environment, you reduce the risk of legal issues

arising from your dog's behavior outside your property.

5. Document training and socialization efforts: Keep a record of your Bullmastiff's training and socialization efforts. This can include attending obedience classes, participating in therapy dog programs, or engaging in any activities that showcase your dog's good behavior and positive interaction with others. Documentation can serve as evidence of your commitment to responsible ownership should any legal disputes arise.

6. Engage in responsible dog ownership practices: Demonstrate responsible dog ownership by adhering to leash laws, cleaning up after your Bullmastiff, and preventing excessive barking or nuisance behavior. By being a considerate and conscientious owner, you contribute to a positive perception of Bullmastiffs and help foster a harmonious relationship with your community.

7. Seek legal advice when needed: If you find yourself facing legal issues or challenges related to your Bullmastiff, don't hesitate to seek legal advice. Consult with an attorney experienced in animal law to understand your rights and explore possible solutions. They can provide guidance and support in navigating complex legal matters and represent your interests if necessary.

Remember, prevention is key when it comes to protecting yourself and your Bullmastiff legally. By being an informed and responsible owner, following local laws and regulations, and seeking legal advice when needed, you can minimize the risk of legal complications and ensure the well-being of your Bullmastiff within the boundaries of the law.

Additionally, consider joining local breed clubs, dog owner associations, or advocacy groups to stay connected with other Bullmastiff owners and stay updated on any legal developments that may affect your dog. By working together and sharing knowledge and experiences, you can strengthen your position and collectively advocate for the fair and just treatment of Bullmastiffs and all dog breeds.

While legal considerations can seem daunting, taking the necessary steps to protect yourself and your Bullmastiff will provide peace of mind and help create a positive and safe environment for all dog owners.

The Influence of Responsible Ownership on Legal Perspectives

Responsible ownership of Bullmastiffs plays a vital role in shaping legal perspectives and creating a positive environment for dog owners and their beloved companions. When owners demonstrate responsible behavior, it helps challenge negative stereotypes, foster understanding, and influence the development of fair and reasonable legislation. In this section, we will explore the influence of responsible ownership on legal perspectives and the positive impact it can have on Bullmastiffs and all dog breeds.

Responsible ownership begins with a commitment to provide proper care, training, and socialization for your Bullmastiff. When you prioritize your dog's well-being, it not only ensures their happiness and health but also reflects positively on the breed as a whole. By consistently demonstrating responsible ownership practices, you contribute to the positive perception of Bullmastiffs and help dispel myths and misconceptions that may surround them.

One of the most significant ways responsible ownership can influence legal perspectives is through education and outreach efforts. Taking an active role in educating others about Bullmastiffs, their temperament, and their needs can help dispel negative stereotypes and promote a more accurate understanding of the breed. By sharing your knowledge and experiences, you can help shape public opinion and influence legislators to consider evidence-based and fair legislation.

Responsible owners also play a crucial role in advocating for breed-neutral laws and regulations that focus on responsible ownership practices rather than discriminatory breed-specific legislation. By joining forces with local breed clubs, dog owner associations, and advocacy groups, you can amplify your voice and contribute to a collective effort to advocate for fair and reasonable laws that protect all dogs and their owners.

Additionally, responsible ownership involves promoting positive interactions between your Bullmastiff and the community. Engaging in therapy dog programs, participating in community events, and promoting responsible dog ownership practices not only showcase the breed's positive qualities but also create opportunities for meaningful interactions with others. These positive experiences can help break down barriers, challenge negative perceptions, and build stronger connections between Bullmastiffs and the community.

Responsible ownership extends to proactive measures that prevent incidents and ensure the safety of your Bullmastiff and others. This includes properly restraining and supervising your dog in public spaces, following leash laws, and addressing any behavioral issues promptly and responsibly. By taking these steps, you demonstrate your commitment to the well-being of your Bullmastiff and actively contribute to a safer and more harmonious community.

Moreover, responsible ownership involves being proactive in addressing any concerns or complaints from neighbors or community members regarding your Bullmastiff. By actively addressing concerns, listening to others' perspectives, and taking appropriate action, you can help alleviate fears and build trust. Engaging in open and respectful dialogue demonstrates that responsible Bullmastiff owners are committed to being good neighbors and contributing positively to the community.

By exemplifying responsible ownership practices, Bullmastiff owners can influence the legal landscape and foster a more inclusive and fair environment for all dog owners. Responsible owners serve as ambassadors for the breed, challenging stereotypes, and proving that Bullmastiffs can be loving, well-behaved companions when given the proper care, training, and socialization.

In conclusion, responsible ownership has a significant influence on legal perspectives surrounding Bullmastiffs and all dog breeds. By demonstrating responsible behavior, educating others, advocating for fair legislation, promoting positive interactions, and addressing concerns proactively, Bullmastiff owners can help shape legal perspectives that prioritize responsible ownership practices and create a safer and more accepting environment for everyone involved. Together, we can promote responsible ownership as the cornerstone of a harmonious and inclusive relationship between Bullmastiffs, their owners, and the community.

Steps to Advocate for Bullmastiffs and Other Breeds

Advocating for Bullmastiffs and other breeds is an important responsibility that can help protect their rights and ensure fair treatment. As a Bullmastiff owner, you have the power to make a difference by taking specific steps to advocate for your beloved companions and create a more inclusive environment for all dogs. In this section, we will explore practical steps you can take to become an effective advocate.

1. Educate yourself: Start by educating yourself about Bullmastiffs and other dog breeds. Learn about their history, characteristics, and unique

qualities. Understanding the breed-specific traits and needs of Bullmastiffs will enable you to articulate their positive attributes and counter any misconceptions or stereotypes.

2. Share knowledge: Share your knowledge about Bullmastiffs and responsible dog ownership with others. Engage in conversations with family, friends, and acquaintances, and provide accurate information about the breed's temperament, exercise requirements, and socialization needs. By sharing your expertise, you can dispel myths and foster a more positive perception of Bullmastiffs.

3. Lead by example: Be a responsible Bullmastiff owner and demonstrate exemplary behavior in your community. Follow local laws and regulations regarding leash laws, licensing, and responsible dog ownership. By practicing responsible ownership, you set a positive example for others to follow and contribute to the overall image of Bullmastiffs as well-behaved and well-cared-for companions.

4. Support breed-specific organizations: Get involved with local Bullmastiff clubs, rescue organizations, or advocacy groups that promote responsible ownership and protect the rights of Bullmastiffs and other breeds. Volunteer your time, participate in events, and support their initiatives to make a meaningful impact within the community.

5. Engage with lawmakers: Reach out to your local legislators and government officials to voice your concerns about breed-specific legislation. Attend town hall meetings, write letters, or participate in public hearings to express your views on the importance of fair and unbiased laws that do not discriminate against specific breeds. By engaging with lawmakers, you can influence their decisions and advocate for the rights of Bullmastiffs and other breeds.

6. Promote responsible ownership: Encourage responsible dog ownership practices within your community. Organize or participate in events that focus on topics such as training, socialization, and responsible breeding. By sharing your experiences and promoting responsible ownership, you can help create a culture of responsible pet ownership that extends beyond Bullmastiffs to all dog breeds.

7. Utilize social media: Leverage the power of social media to advocate for Bullmastiffs and other breeds. Share informative posts, educational resources, and heartwarming stories about Bullmastiffs to raise awareness and challenge negative stereotypes. Engage with like-minded individuals and organizations to amplify your message and reach a wider audience.

8. Collaborate with local authorities: Work collaboratively with local animal control officers, shelters, and law enforcement agencies

to promote responsible dog ownership. Participate in community programs that focus on responsible pet ownership, such as microchipping and spaying/neutering campaigns. By building positive relationships with authorities, you can foster a cooperative environment that prioritizes the well-being of Bullmastiffs and all dogs.

9. Support legislation and initiatives: Stay informed about proposed legislation that impacts dog ownership and breed-specific legislation. Support initiatives that promote fair and evidence-based regulations aimed at improving the welfare of all dogs. Participate in petition drives, attend public meetings, and write letters to your elected representatives to voice your support for responsible ownership practices and equal treatment for all breeds.

10. Be an ambassador: Serve as an ambassador for Bullmastiffs and responsible dog ownership. Engage in positive interactions with others, allowing them to experience the gentle and loving nature of Bullmastiffs firsthand. Encourage potential dog owners to consider adoption from shelters or reputable breeders and emphasize the importance of responsible pet ownership.

Remember, advocacy is an ongoing process that requires perseverance and dedication. By taking these steps, you can be a powerful advocate for Bullmastiffs and other breeds, making a positive impact on their welfare and the overall perception of dogs in society. Together, we can create a more inclusive and compassionate environment for all our beloved companions.

CHAPTER 11: BULLMASTIFFS IN WORK AND SPORTS

Bullmastiffs, with their imposing size and impressive capabilities, have proven themselves to be versatile and capable working dogs. In this chapter, we will explore the various roles and opportunities for Bullmastiffs in work and sports. From protection work to therapy dog programs, Bullmastiffs can excel in a wide range of activities. Let's delve into the exciting world of Bullmastiffs in work and sports!

Bullmastiffs have a natural instinct to protect and guard, making them well-suited for roles in protection work. They possess an innate sense of loyalty and dedication to their families, which can be channeled into training for personal protection, home security, or even working in law enforcement. With the proper training and guidance, Bullmastiffs can become formidable protectors while maintaining their calm and composed demeanor.

Another area where Bullmastiffs excel is in therapy work. Their gentle and affectionate nature, combined with their imposing presence, can bring comfort and joy to individuals in need. Bullmastiffs have a remarkable ability to provide emotional support and companionship to those going through difficult times, whether it's in hospitals, nursing homes, or schools. Their calm and reassuring presence can make a significant difference in people's lives.

Additionally, Bullmastiffs can participate in various dog sports and competitions. Their athleticism and strength make them suitable candidates for activities such as obedience trials, agility courses, and weight pulling. With their intelligence and willingness to please, Bullmastiffs can be trained to navigate obstacles, follow commands, and showcase their physical abilities in a fun and competitive environment.

For those interested in working with animals, Bullmastiffs can also be trained for search and rescue operations. Their keen sense of smell and endurance make them valuable assets in locating missing persons or providing assistance during natural disasters. With their size and determination, Bullmastiffs can navigate challenging terrains and work alongside search and rescue teams to help save lives.

It's important to note that engaging Bullmastiffs in work and sports requires proper training, socialization, and guidance from experienced handlers. Working and sporting activities should always prioritize the well-being and safety of both the dog and the handlers involved. It's crucial to work with trainers who have experience with large and powerful breeds, ensuring that the training methods are positive, balanced, and suited to the individual dog's temperament and abilities.

Whether it's protecting, providing therapy, competing in sports, or participating in search and rescue operations, Bullmastiffs have the potential to excel and thrive in various work and sports settings. It's essential to recognize and appreciate their unique strengths and abilities while providing them with the necessary training and opportunities to fulfill their potential.

If you're considering involving your Bullmastiff in work or sports, consult with experienced trainers, breed-specific organizations, and fellow Bullmastiff owners to gather information, guidance, and support.

Engaging your Bullmastiff in these activities can enhance their physical and mental well-being, strengthen the bond between you, and allow them to showcase their impressive abilities.

Remember to always prioritize your Bullmastiff's health, happiness, and welfare throughout their participation in work and sports. By providing them with the appropriate training, care, and support, you can help them fulfill their potential while ensuring their overall well-being.

Breed Suitability for Work and Sports

When considering involving Bullmastiffs in work and sports, it's important to understand their breed suitability for different activities. While Bullmastiffs may not be the first breed that comes to mind when thinking about working dogs or sports, they possess unique qualities that make them well-suited for specific roles.

One of the primary factors that determine breed suitability is their physical attributes. Bullmastiffs are large, muscular dogs with a strong build. Their impressive size and strength enable them to perform physically demanding tasks and excel in activities that require power and endurance. Whether it's pulling weights in weight-pulling competitions or traversing agility courses, Bullmastiffs have the physical prowess to compete.

Furthermore, Bullmastiffs have a natural instinct to protect and guard their families and territory. This instinct can be harnessed and channeled into protection work, where they can excel as personal protection dogs or in roles related to home security. With proper training and guidance, Bullmastiffs can utilize their natural instincts to become formidable protectors while maintaining their calm and composed demeanor.

In terms of temperament, Bullmastiffs are known for their loyalty, devotion, and gentle nature. These qualities make them excellent candidates for therapy work, where they can provide emotional support and comfort to individuals in need.

Their calm and reassuring presence can have a positive impact on patients in hospitals, residents in nursing homes, or children in schools. Bullmastiffs

have an uncanny ability to connect with people on an emotional level, bringing joy and companionship wherever they go.
It's essential to consider the individual characteristics and personality of each Bullmastiff when determining their suitability for specific work or sports.

While the breed, in general, possesses certain traits, individual variations exist. Some Bullmastiffs may display a stronger drive and enthusiasm for certain activities, while others may lean more towards a laid-back and easygoing nature. Evaluating the temperament, energy level, and drive of your Bullmastiff will help you identify which activities align with their natural abilities and interests.

When engaging Bullmastiffs in work and sports, it's crucial to provide proper training, socialization, and guidance from experienced handlers. Working and sporting activities should prioritize the safety and well-being of both the dog and the handlers involved. Training methods should be positive, balanced, and tailored to the individual dog's temperament and abilities. By working with experienced trainers and organizations, you can ensure that your Bullmastiff receives the appropriate training and support to excel in their chosen field.

In conclusion, Bullmastiffs possess unique qualities that make them suitable for specific work and sports activities. Their physical attributes, protective instincts, loyalty, and gentle nature contribute to their potential success in various roles. By understanding the breed suitability for different activities and considering the individual characteristics of your Bullmastiff, you can find fulfilling and enjoyable work or sports opportunities that cater to their natural abilities and interests.

Bullmastiffs in Protection Work

Bullmastiffs possess inherent protective instincts that make them well-suited for roles in protection work. With their imposing size, strength, and loyalty, they can excel in various aspects of protection and security. In this section, we will explore the fascinating world of Bullmastiffs in protection work and how they contribute to maintaining safety and peace.

One of the key qualities that sets Bullmastiffs apart in protection work is their natural instinct to protect their families and territory. They have a strong sense of loyalty and devotion, and their inherent protective nature can be channeled through proper training and guidance. Bullmastiffs are known for their watchful and alert nature, always on the lookout for any potential threats or intruders.

In protection work, Bullmastiffs can serve as personal protection dogs, home security dogs, or even in roles related to law enforcement. Their imposing presence alone is often enough to deter potential intruders.

Bullmastiffs have a commanding appearance that commands respect and gives a sense of security to those around them. Their sheer size and strength, coupled with their protective instincts, make them a force to be reckoned with when it comes to safeguarding their loved ones and property.

To excel in protection work, Bullmastiffs require appropriate training from experienced handlers. The training process should focus on developing their protective instincts, refining their obedience skills, and enhancing their ability to assess potential threats. It's important to strike a balance between their protective nature and their ability to remain calm and composed in various situations.

Proper socialization is also crucial in protection work. Bullmastiffs need to be exposed to different environments, people, and scenarios to ensure they can distinguish between genuine threats and harmless situations. Socializing them from a young age helps them develop the necessary confidence, discernment, and self-control required for effective protection work.

It's important to note that Bullmastiffs are typically not aggressive by nature. Their role in protection work is more about deterrence and controlled response rather than actively seeking confrontation. They are known for their discernment and the ability to assess situations before taking action. This discerning nature makes them reliable and trustworthy protectors.

When considering involving Bullmastiffs in protection work, it's crucial to work with experienced trainers who specialize in working breeds. These professionals can guide you in understanding the unique training requirements and techniques specific to Bullmastiffs. They will help you develop a strong bond with your Bullmastiff, instilling trust and ensuring effective communication during protection work.

In conclusion, Bullmastiffs have the potential to excel in protection work due to their natural protective instincts, imposing presence, and loyalty. Their role as protectors involves using their size, strength, and discernment to ensure the safety of their families and property. With proper training, socialization, and guidance, Bullmastiffs can fulfill their potential as reliable and effective protectors in various protection work settings.

Training for Sports and Work

Training is an essential aspect of preparing Bullmastiffs for sports and work activities. Whether it's obedience trials, agility courses, or specialized work tasks, a well-trained Bullmastiff can showcase their abilities and excel in their chosen field. In this section, we will explore the importance of training and the key considerations for preparing Bullmastiffs for sports and work.

The foundation of training begins with basic obedience. Teaching Bullmastiffs essential commands such as sit, stay, come, and heel establishes a line of communication between the dog and the handler.

This communication is vital during sports and work activities, where precise commands and prompt responses are required. Basic obedience training also helps build a strong bond between the Bullmastiff and their handler, fostering trust and cooperation.

As Bullmastiffs progress in their training journey, specialized training tailored to their chosen sports or work tasks becomes necessary.

Different activities require specific skills and behaviors, and it's important to focus on developing those skills through targeted training. For example, agility training may involve teaching the Bullmastiff to navigate through obstacles, follow directional cues, and maintain speed and accuracy. Protection work training, on the other hand, may include bite work, controlled aggression, and response to various commands.

Positive reinforcement is a key training method that works well with Bullmastiffs. These gentle giants respond favorably to praise, treats, and rewards when they exhibit desired behaviors. Positive reinforcement creates a positive association with training, making it an enjoyable experience for both the dog and the handler. Consistency, patience, and clear communication are essential when using positive reinforcement to shape Bullmastiffs' behavior and skills.

Working with an experienced trainer who specializes in working breeds, sports, or specific work tasks can greatly enhance the training process. These trainers have the expertise to tailor the training methods to suit the Bullmastiff's temperament, capabilities, and the requirements of the chosen activity. They can provide valuable guidance, techniques, and insights to maximize the Bullmastiff's potential.

Training should be conducted in a safe and controlled environment. It's important to ensure that the training area is secure and free from distractions that may hinder the Bullmastiff's focus. Gradual progression is key, starting with simple exercises and gradually increasing the difficulty level as the Bullmastiff becomes more proficient. Regular training sessions, consistency, and repetition help solidify learned behaviors and improve performance.

In addition to physical training, mental stimulation is vital for Bullmastiffs engaged in sports and work. Mental exercises such as problem-solving activities, scent work, and interactive games help keep their minds sharp and engaged. Mental stimulation not only enhances their cognitive abilities but also prevents boredom, which can lead to destructive behaviors.

It's important to remember that training for sports and work should be a positive and enjoyable experience for both the Bullmastiff and the handler. Building a strong bond based on trust and understanding is crucial. Patience, encouragement, and celebrating small victories along the way contribute to a successful training journey.

In conclusion, training plays a pivotal role in preparing Bullmastiffs for sports and work activities. Basic obedience provides a foundation for effective communication, while specialized training hones their skills for specific tasks. Positive reinforcement, consistency, and the guidance of experienced trainers are key elements in the training process.

Mental stimulation complements physical training, keeping Bullmastiffs engaged and motivated. By investing time and effort in training, Bullmastiffs can unlock their full potential and thrive in the world of sports and work.

Impact of Work and Sports on a Bullmastiff's Wellbeing

Engaging Bullmastiffs in work and sports activities can have a significant impact on their overall wellbeing. These activities provide mental and physical stimulation, promote a healthy lifestyle, and foster a strong bond between the Bullmastiff and their handler. In this section, we will explore the positive effects of work and sports on a Bullmastiff's wellbeing and the considerations to ensure their health and happiness.

Physical exercise is a vital component of a Bullmastiff's wellbeing. Engaging in sports and work activities allows them to burn off excess energy, maintain a healthy weight, and improve cardiovascular health. Regular physical exercise helps prevent obesity, which is a common issue among dogs that do not receive adequate exercise. It also promotes strong muscles, joints, and overall physical fitness.

Sports and work activities also provide mental stimulation for Bullmastiffs. These intelligent dogs thrive on mental challenges and problem-solving tasks. Engaging their minds through training exercises, problem-solving games, and interactive activities keeps them mentally sharp and fulfilled. Mental stimulation helps prevent boredom, which can lead to destructive behaviors such as chewing or excessive barking.

Furthermore, participating in work and sports activities strengthens the bond between Bullmastiffs and their handlers. These activities require teamwork, trust, and effective communication. The shared experiences, training sessions, and accomplishments create a strong sense of partnership and enhance the bond between the Bullmastiff and their handler. The deep connection developed through work and sports activities contributes to a happier and more fulfilling life for both the dog and the handler.

However, it's important to consider the impact of work and sports on a Bullmastiff's physical and mental health. While these activities are beneficial, they should be tailored to the individual dog's capabilities, age, and health condition. Pushing a Bullmastiff beyond their physical limitations or engaging in activities that are not suitable for their age or health can lead to injuries or undue stress.

It's crucial to strike a balance between exercise, rest, and recovery. Overexertion or inadequate rest can result in fatigue, muscle strain, or even joint issues. Providing sufficient time for rest and recovery allows the Bullmastiff's body to heal and rebuild, ensuring their long-term health and wellbeing.

Regular veterinary check-ups are essential to monitor a Bullmastiff's health and address any potential issues. These visits allow the veterinarian to assess the dog's physical condition, provide preventive care, and identify any underlying health concerns that may affect their ability to engage in work and sports activities. It's important to follow the veterinarian's recommendations regarding vaccinations, parasite prevention, and overall health management.

In addition, nutrition plays a vital role in supporting a Bullmastiff's overall wellbeing. Proper nutrition helps maintain their energy levels, supports healthy growth and development, and provides the necessary nutrients for their muscles, joints, and overall health. Consultation with a veterinarian or a canine nutritionist can help determine the appropriate diet for a Bullmastiff engaged in work and sports activities.

Lastly, it's important to listen to the Bullmastiff's body language and cues during work and sports activities. Pay attention to signs of fatigue, stress, or discomfort. If the Bullmastiff shows signs of exhaustion or seems disinterested, it may be necessary to adjust the intensity or duration of the activity. Their safety and wellbeing should always be the top priority.

In conclusion, work and sports activities have a positive impact on a Bullmastiff's overall wellbeing. They provide physical exercise, mental stimulation, and strengthen the bond between the dog and their handler.

However, it's essential to consider the individual dog's capabilities, age, and health when engaging them in these activities. Striking a balance between exercise, rest, and recovery, regular veterinary care, proper nutrition, and attentive observation ensure the

Bullmastiff's health, happiness, and longevity in their work and sports pursuits.

Famous Bullmastiffs in Work and Sports

Throughout history, there have been notable Bullmastiffs that have made their mark in various work and sports endeavors. These exceptional dogs have showcased the breed's capabilities, intelligence, and dedication. In this section, we will explore some famous Bullmastiffs who have achieved recognition and made significant contributions in work and sports.

One famous Bullmastiff that stands out is "Ceasar," a remarkable therapy dog who provided comfort and support to patients in hospitals and nursing homes. With his gentle demeanor and empathetic nature, Ceasar touched the lives of many individuals, bringing smiles and companionship to those in need. His work as a therapy dog highlighted the Bullmastiff's innate ability to provide emotional support and make a positive impact in people's lives.

In the field of search and rescue, "Max" gained recognition for his exceptional tracking skills and life-saving abilities. Max was known for his determination, keen sense of smell, and unwavering commitment to locating missing individuals. He played a crucial role in numerous successful search and rescue operations, earning him the admiration and respect of his handlers and the community.

In the world of competitive obedience, "Bella" became a household name. With her impressive training and exceptional performance, Bella captured the hearts of judges and audiences alike. Her precision, responsiveness, and graceful movements demonstrated the Bullmastiff's ability to excel in obedience trials. Bella's success in competitive obedience highlighted the breed's intelligence, trainability, and desire to please.

The Bullmastiff's protective instincts have also been showcased in the field of personal protection and security. "Thor" gained recognition as a top-notch security dog, providing a formidable deterrent and a reliable protector. With his imposing presence, alertness, and unwavering loyalty, Thor served as a reliable guardian, ensuring the safety and security of his owners and their property.

Another Bullmastiff that left a lasting legacy is "Apollo," a highly skilled tracking dog in law enforcement. Apollo's exceptional tracking abilities, combined with his unwavering focus and determination, made him an invaluable asset in locating and apprehending suspects. His contributions in the field of tracking demonstrated the Bullmastiff's intelligence, scenting capabilities, and versatility in law enforcement work.

These famous Bullmastiffs serve as inspiring examples of the breed's capabilities and the impact they can make in various work and sports endeavors. They showcase the Bullmastiff's intelligence, loyalty, trainability, and versatility, which are essential traits in achieving success in these fields.

It's important to note that these exceptional Bullmastiffs are the result of dedicated training, consistent handling, and the strong bond between the dogs and their handlers. Behind their achievements lies the hard work, commitment, and passion of their owners and trainers.

While not every Bullmastiff will reach the same level of fame or recognition as these notable examples, every Bullmastiff has the potential to excel in their own unique way. Whether it's in therapy work, search and rescue, competitive obedience, or other activities, each Bullmastiff has their individual strengths and talents that can be nurtured and developed.

In conclusion, the stories of famous Bullmastiffs in work and sports demonstrate the breed's remarkable abilities and contributions. They serve as inspirations for Bullmastiff owners and enthusiasts, showcasing what can be accomplished with dedication, training, and a strong bond between a Bullmastiff and their handler.

These exceptional dogs exemplify the Bullmastiff's potential to make a positive impact in various work and sports fields and further solidify their reputation as remarkable and versatile canine companions.

Potential Careers for Bullmastiffs

Bullmastiffs possess a unique set of characteristics and abilities that make them well-suited for various careers and roles. Their intelligence, loyalty, and physical prowess open doors to a wide range of professions where they can excel and make a meaningful impact. In this section, we will explore some potential careers for Bullmastiffs and the contributions they can make in these fields.

One career path that Bullmastiffs often excel in is that of a service dog. With their gentle and patient nature, they can be trained to assist individuals with disabilities. Whether it's guiding individuals with visual impairments, alerting to sounds for the hearing-impaired, or providing support to those with mobility challenges, Bullmastiffs can be reliable and devoted service companions, helping their handlers navigate the world with greater independence.

Bullmastiffs also have a strong protective instinct, making them well-suited for roles in security and protection work. Their imposing presence and alertness make them excellent guard dogs, providing a visible deterrent and a reliable defense against intruders. Their loyalty and courage make them dependable partners in protecting property, assets, and the safety of their owners.

In the field of search and rescue, Bullmastiffs can use their exceptional tracking abilities and scenting capabilities to locate missing individuals. Their determination, focus, and strong sense of smell enable them to navigate through various terrains and conditions, assisting search and rescue teams in locating lost or trapped individuals.

Therapy work is another avenue where Bullmastiffs can shine. Their calm and gentle demeanor, coupled with their inherent empathy, make them excellent therapy dogs. They can provide comfort, emotional support, and companionship to individuals in hospitals, nursing homes, or other therapeutic settings. Their mere presence can bring joy, alleviate stress, and make a positive difference in the lives of those they interact with.

Bullmastiffs can also excel in competitive obedience and dog sports. Their intelligence, trainability, and willingness to please make them ideal candidates for obedience trials, agility competitions, and other dog sports. Their size and strength can be harnessed in activities such as weight pulling or carting, showcasing their power and athleticism.

In addition to these specific career paths, Bullmastiffs can also serve as valuable members of search and rescue teams, law enforcement agencies, and even as actors in the entertainment industry. Their versatility and adaptability make them capable of taking on a variety of roles and responsibilities, always displaying their trademark loyalty and dedication.

It's important to note that pursuing a career for a Bullmastiff requires proper training, socialization, and ongoing education. Each career path has its specific requirements and training protocols, and it's essential to work with experienced trainers and handlers who understand the unique needs and abilities of the breed.

Furthermore, not every Bullmastiff will have the aptitude or interest in pursuing a specific career. Each dog is an individual with their own strengths and preferences. It's crucial to assess the dog's temperament, physical capabilities, and willingness to engage in specific activities before committing to a particular career path. Not all Bullmastiffs will excel in every career, but with the right guidance and support, they can find their niche and make a meaningful contribution in their chosen field.

In conclusion, Bullmastiffs have the potential to thrive in various careers and roles. Their intelligence, loyalty, and physical abilities make them valuable assets in service work, security and protection, search and rescue, therapy, competitive obedience, and other fields.

The key is to recognize their unique strengths, provide proper training and socialization, and nurture their innate abilities. With the right guidance and opportunities, Bullmastiffs can lead fulfilling and impactful careers while demonstrating their exceptional qualities and making a positive difference in the lives of those they serve.

CHAPTER 12: LIFE WITH A BULLMASTIFF

Owning a Bullmastiff is a rewarding and fulfilling experience. These gentle giants bring joy, loyalty, and companionship into our lives. In this chapter, we will explore what it's like to live with a Bullmastiff, the adjustments needed, the financial aspect of ownership, traveling with your Bullmastiff, preparing your home, and how to cope with loss and grief.

Living with a Bullmastiff requires some adjustments to accommodate their specific needs and characteristics. Due to their size, it's important to ensure that you have enough space in your home and yard for them to move comfortably. They may also have special dietary requirements, so it's essential to provide them with a balanced and nutritious diet that supports their health and well-being.

Financially, owning a Bullmastiff entails certain expenses. Beyond the initial cost of acquiring a Bullmastiff from a reputable breeder, there are ongoing expenses such as food, veterinary care, grooming supplies, and potential training classes. It's crucial to budget and plan for these expenses to ensure that your Bullmastiff receives the care they need throughout their life.

When it comes to traveling with your Bullmastiff, it's important to make appropriate arrangements. Bullmastiffs may not be the best candidates for long trips or air travel due to their size and potential stress associated with unfamiliar environments. However, with proper planning, you can still enjoy road trips and vacations together. Ensure that you have suitable accommodations that can accommodate your Bullmastiff's size and comfort needs.

Preparing your home for a Bullmastiff involves creating a safe and welcoming environment. Securely fenced yards are essential to prevent them from wandering off and to ensure their safety. Inside the house, you may need to make adjustments to protect valuable or delicate items from an exuberant wagging tail. Providing a comfortable bed or crate where your Bullmastiff can rest is also important for their well-being.

One aspect of owning a Bullmastiff that requires sensitivity is dealing with loss and grief. Bullmastiffs are beloved family members, and their lifespan, although generally long for their size, is still limited. Coping with the loss of a Bullmastiff can be challenging and emotionally painful. It's important to give yourself time to grieve and seek support from loved ones or even support groups who understand the unique bond we share with our furry companions.

Despite the challenges and adjustments, life with a Bullmastiff is filled with love, loyalty, and unforgettable moments. Their gentle and affectionate nature makes them wonderful family pets and companions. Whether it's the joy of their warm greetings when you come home, their comforting presence during difficult times, or the fun and laughter they bring to everyday life, Bullmastiffs have a way of touching our hearts and making our lives richer.

The bond between a Bullmastiff and their owner is a special one. They are incredibly loyal and devoted, always ready to stand by your side and offer their unconditional love. Their protective instincts make them natural guardians, providing a sense of security and peace of mind.

In conclusion, life with a Bullmastiff is a unique and fulfilling experience. From the adjustments needed to the financial responsibilities, traveling together, preparing your home, and navigating the journey of loss and grief, every aspect is an opportunity to deepen the bond and create cherished memories.

The love and companionship of a Bullmastiff are truly priceless, and the joy they bring to our lives is immeasurable. Embrace the journey with your Bullmastiff and savor every moment together.

The Bullmastiff as a Family Pet

The Bullmastiff is an exceptional breed that thrives in a family environment. They are renowned for their gentle and affectionate nature, making them wonderful companions for individuals of all ages, from children to seniors. In this section, we will explore why Bullmastiffs are well-suited as family pets and the unique qualities they bring to a household.

One of the defining characteristics of Bullmastiffs is their inherent love for their family. They form deep bonds with their human companions and are known for their unwavering loyalty. Your Bullmastiff will become an integral part of your family, showering you with affection and always being there to provide comfort and companionship.

Bullmastiffs are renowned for their patience and gentleness, especially with children. They have a natural protective instinct and will go to great lengths to ensure the safety of their loved ones. They are known to be tolerant and calm, even in the face of energetic play or clumsy interactions. This makes them an ideal choice for families with young children, providing a reliable and loving presence.

Additionally, Bullmastiffs are highly adaptable to various living situations. Whether you live in a spacious house with a backyard or a cozy apartment, they can adapt to their environment as long as their needs for exercise, mental stimulation, and companionship are met. However, it's important to note that due to their size, Bullmastiffs may require more space compared to smaller breeds.

Another advantage of Bullmastiffs as family pets is their laid-back and easygoing nature. They are not known for being overly demanding or high-strung. They enjoy spending quality time with their family, whether it's participating in family activities, going for leisurely walks, or simply lounging together. Their calm demeanor creates a sense of tranquility within the household, promoting a peaceful and harmonious atmosphere.

Bullmastiffs are also known to be excellent with other pets. With proper socialization and introductions, they can coexist harmoniously with cats, small animals, and other dogs. Their friendly and tolerant nature allows them to form strong bonds with their furry counterparts, fostering a harmonious multi-pet household.

While Bullmastiffs are known for their calm and gentle temperament, it's important to provide them with proper training and socialization from an early age. Basic obedience training and positive reinforcement techniques can help mold them into well-mannered and obedient family members. It's essential to establish clear boundaries and consistent rules to ensure a harmonious coexistence between your Bullmastiff and the rest of the family.

In summary, the Bullmastiff is an excellent choice for a family pet. Their loving nature, loyalty, and gentle temperament make them a natural fit for families of all sizes.

They thrive in an environment where they are given love, attention, and ample opportunities for exercise and mental stimulation. Whether you're seeking a cuddly companion for your children or a faithful friend for yourself, the Bullmastiff is sure to bring joy, love, and a sense of security to your family life.

Lifestyle Adjustments Needed for Owning a Bullmastiff

Owning a Bullmastiff requires certain lifestyle adjustments to ensure the well-being and happiness of both you and your furry companion. In this section, we will discuss the specific adjustments you may need to make when bringing a Bullmastiff into your home and family.

First and foremost, Bullmastiffs are a large breed, and their size alone necessitates some accommodations. They require ample space to move around comfortably, both indoors and outdoors. Before bringing a Bullmastiff into your home, consider the size of your living quarters and whether you have a suitable yard or access to nearby parks or open spaces where your Bullmastiff can exercise and stretch their legs. Adequate space is essential for their physical and mental well-being.

Additionally, due to their large size, Bullmastiffs may inadvertently knock over or damage fragile items in your home. It's important to make adjustments to your living space to minimize the risk of accidents. Secure valuable or delicate items out of their reach, and consider providing them with a designated space or bed where they can rest comfortably without causing disruptions.

Another lifestyle adjustment to consider is the level of exercise Bullmastiffs require. Despite their calm demeanor, they are an active breed that needs regular physical activity to stay healthy and maintain a balanced temperament. Daily walks, interactive play sessions, and ample opportunities to stretch their muscles are crucial for their overall well-being. As a Bullmastiff owner, you should be prepared to devote time and energy to meeting their exercise needs.

Bullmastiffs are known for their affinity for human companionship and dislike being left alone for long periods. They thrive when they are included as part of the family and given ample attention and social interaction. If your lifestyle requires long hours away from home, it's important to consider whether you can provide them with the companionship and mental stimulation they need.

You may need to arrange for a trusted pet sitter, doggy daycare, or enlist the help of family members or friends to ensure your Bullmastiff receives the necessary attention and care.

Furthermore, Bullmastiffs have a protective instinct and are naturally inclined to guard their loved ones. While this can be an asset, it's essential to guide and manage their protective behavior through proper training and socialization.

This includes exposing them to various people, animals, and environments from an early age, as well as teaching them appropriate responses to different situations. This adjustment will help your Bullmastiff become a well-rounded and well-behaved member of your family.

Lastly, owning a Bullmastiff requires being mindful of their specific health needs. Regular veterinary check-ups, a balanced diet, and proper grooming are vital components of their care. It's important to establish a relationship with a reputable veterinarian who has experience with large breeds and can provide guidance on health-related matters.

In conclusion, owning a Bullmastiff comes with certain lifestyle adjustments. Providing them with ample space, meeting their exercise needs, ensuring social interaction, and managing their protective instincts through training and socialization are all important considerations.

By making these adjustments, you will create a nurturing and fulfilling environment for your Bullmastiff, allowing them to thrive and become an integral part of your family life.

The Financial Aspect of Bullmastiff Ownership

When considering owning a Bullmastiff, it's important to be aware of the financial responsibilities that come along with it. In this section, we will discuss the financial aspects of Bullmastiff ownership and the various expenses you can expect to encounter throughout their lifetime.

First and foremost, the initial cost of acquiring a Bullmastiff can vary depending on factors such as the breeder's reputation, pedigree, and the demand for the breed. Reputable breeders who prioritize the health and well-being of their dogs may charge higher prices. It's essential to invest in a Bullmastiff from a responsible breeder to ensure you're getting a healthy and well-socialized puppy.

Once you bring your Bullmastiff home, there are several immediate expenses to consider. These may include purchasing essential supplies such as food and water bowls, a comfortable bed or crate, collar and leash, grooming tools, and toys. You may also need to budget for initial vaccinations, microchipping, and spaying or neutering, if not already done by the breeder.

Ongoing expenses related to Bullmastiff ownership include high-quality dog food that meets their nutritional needs, routine veterinary care, and preventive medications such as flea and tick treatments, heartworm preventives, and annual vaccinations. It's important to budget for regular check-ups, dental care, and any potential health issues that may arise as your Bullmastiff ages. Additionally, grooming expenses should be taken into account, including professional grooming or necessary grooming supplies if you choose to groom your Bullmastiff at home.

Another financial consideration is training and socialization. While Bullmastiffs are generally well-behaved, investing in basic obedience training and socialization classes is essential for their well-being and the safety of others. Training helps establish a strong bond between you and your Bullmastiff while ensuring they have good manners and respond to commands reliably.

Furthermore, Bullmastiffs are a large breed and may require more food compared to smaller dogs. It's important to provide them with a balanced and nutritious diet to support their growth, overall health, and energy levels. The cost of high-quality dog food, treats, and supplements should be factored into your budget.

Emergency veterinary care is another potential expense to consider. While we hope your Bullmastiff remains healthy throughout their life, unexpected accidents or illnesses can occur. It's wise to set aside funds or consider pet insurance to help cover the cost of emergency veterinary care should the need arise.

Lastly, it's important to remember that Bullmastiffs are a long-lived breed, typically living between 8 and 10 years. As they age, they may require additional medical care, such as specialized diets, medications for joint health, and ongoing veterinary monitoring. It's important to be prepared for these additional expenses as your Bullmastiff enters their senior years.

In summary, owning a Bullmastiff comes with financial responsibilities. Beyond the initial cost of acquiring your dog, there are ongoing expenses to consider, including food, veterinary care, grooming, training, and potential emergency veterinary expenses.

By budgeting and planning for these financial aspects, you can ensure that your Bullmastiff receives the care and support they need throughout their life, while providing you with the joy and companionship that comes with owning this wonderful breed.

Tips for Traveling with a Bullmastiff

Traveling with your Bullmastiff can be a rewarding and enjoyable experience, but it requires some extra preparation and consideration. In this section, we will provide you with helpful tips to make traveling with your Bullmastiff a smooth and stress-free experience. First and foremost, it's essential to ensure your Bullmastiff's safety and comfort during travel.

If you're traveling by car, invest in a sturdy and well-ventilated crate or a spacious travel harness that will keep your Bullmastiff secure and prevent them from moving around too much while driving. Make sure the crate or harness is properly secured in the vehicle to avoid any accidents or sudden movements.

If you're planning to travel by air, check with the airline about their specific requirements for traveling with large dog breeds. Each airline may have different regulations regarding crate size, documentation, and restrictions, so it's important to familiarize yourself with their policies well in advance. Additionally, consider booking a direct flight whenever possible to minimize travel time and reduce stress for your Bullmastiff.

Before embarking on your journey, it's crucial to acclimate your Bullmastiff to their travel crate or harness. Start by introducing them to it gradually, allowing them to explore and associate it with positive experiences such as treats and praise. Gradually increase the duration of time they spend in the crate or wearing the harness to help them feel more comfortable and relaxed during travel.

Pack all the necessary supplies for your Bullmastiff's well-being during the trip. This includes their regular food, water, food and water bowls, medication if applicable, favorite toys or comfort items, and any other essentials they may need. Having familiar items with them will help provide a sense of security and make them feel more at ease in unfamiliar surroundings.

During the journey, it's important to take regular breaks for your Bullmastiff to stretch their legs, relieve themselves, and have a drink of water. Plan your stops in advance and look for pet-friendly rest areas or parks where your Bullmastiff can safely exercise and take a break from the confines of the car.

Research and book pet-friendly accommodations in advance to ensure a smooth and comfortable stay. Many hotels and vacation rentals welcome dogs, but it's important to check their pet policies, any size restrictions, and whether there are any additional fees or requirements. Also, consider the availability of nearby walking areas or parks where your Bullmastiff can get some exercise and fresh air.

When traveling with your Bullmastiff, it's important to be a responsible pet owner and respectful of others. Always clean up after your dog and dispose of waste properly. Keep your Bullmastiff on a leash whenever necessary, and be mindful of local rules and regulations regarding dogs in public spaces.

Lastly, remember to be patient and understanding during the travel experience. Your Bullmastiff may feel a bit anxious or stressed in new environments, so provide them with reassurance and a calm presence. Stick to their regular routine as much as possible, including feeding and exercise schedules, to provide them with a sense of familiarity and comfort.

By following these tips, you can ensure that traveling with your Bullmastiff is a positive experience for both you and your furry companion. Whether you're embarking on a road trip or flying to a new destination, with proper preparation and care, you can create wonderful memories together and enjoy exploring the world with your beloved Bullmastiff by your side.

Preparing Your Home for a Bullmastiff
Bringing a Bullmastiff into your home is an exciting and fulfilling experience. However, it's important to make some adjustments to ensure that your home is safe and suitable for your new furry family member. In this section, we will provide you with helpful tips on preparing your home for a Bullmastiff.

First and foremost, Bullmastiffs are known for their size and strength, so it's important to create a designated space for them that is both comfortable and secure. Consider designating a specific area in your home where your Bullmastiff can have their bed, toys, and access to water. This area should be easily accessible and provide enough room for them to move around comfortably.

Bullmastiffs are prone to certain health issues, particularly joint problems. Providing a comfortable and supportive bed is essential to ensure their well-being. Invest in a high-quality orthopedic dog bed that offers ample cushioning and support for their joints. This will help prevent discomfort and potential joint issues as they age.

Since Bullmastiffs are a large and powerful breed, it's important to secure your home to prevent any potential accidents or damage. Ensure that all doors and gates leading outside are securely fenced and latched to prevent your Bullmastiff from wandering off. Consider installing baby gates or pet gates in areas where you want to restrict their access, such as staircases or certain rooms.

Bullmastiffs are also known to be droolers, so it's a good idea to have some drool towels or absorbent mats handy in areas where they spend a lot of time. This will help keep your floors and furniture clean and prevent any slipping accidents due to wet surfaces.

Take a look around your home and identify any potential hazards or items that could be tempting for your Bullmastiff to chew on. Secure electrical cords, move toxic plants out of their reach, and keep household chemicals and medications safely stored in cabinets. It's also a good idea to invest in some sturdy and durable chew toys to redirect their chewing instincts away from household items.

Since Bullmastiffs are a brachycephalic breed, meaning they have a shorter snout, they can be sensitive to extreme temperatures. Ensure that your home is adequately climate-controlled, especially during hot summers and cold winters. Provide them with a cool and comfortable space during the warmer months and a warm area during the colder months.

When introducing a Bullmastiff to your home, it's important to establish clear rules and boundaries from the start. Consistency is key in their training and development. Set expectations regarding areas they are allowed to access, furniture they can or cannot be on, and any house rules you want them to follow.

With proper guidance and training, your Bullmastiff will quickly understand and respect these boundaries. Lastly, don't forget to stock up on essential supplies before bringing your Bullmastiff home. This includes food and water bowls, a sturdy leash and collar, ID tags with your contact information, grooming supplies, and appropriate toys and chew items. Having these items readily available will help your Bullmastiff settle into their new home with ease.

By following these tips, you can ensure that your home is prepared to welcome your Bullmastiff with open arms. Creating a safe and comfortable environment will not only enhance their well-being but also strengthen the bond between you and your new furry companion. Get ready for endless love, joy, and unforgettable moments with your Bullmastiff in your lovingly prepared home.

THE BULLMASTIFF

Stories and Experiences from Bullmastiff Owners

One of the joys of owning a Bullmastiff is being part of a community of dedicated and passionate Bullmastiff owners. Their stories and experiences can provide valuable insights and a deeper understanding of what it's like to share your life with this amazing breed. In this section, we'll share some heartwarming and enlightening stories from Bullmastiff owners.

Emily, a Bullmastiff enthusiast, shares her story: "When I first brought my Bullmastiff, Max, home, I was instantly captivated by his gentle nature and unwavering loyalty. Max quickly became a beloved member of our family.

His calm demeanor and friendly personality have brought so much joy to our lives. Whether we're cuddling on the couch or going for long walks, Max's presence brings a sense of comfort and companionship that is truly irreplaceable."

John, another Bullmastiff owner, recalls an unforgettable experience: "One day, while I was out for a walk with my Bullmastiff, Bella, we encountered a situation that showcased her protective instincts. As we passed a construction site, a loud noise startled me, and I stumbled. Instantly, Bella positioned herself between me and the source of the noise, standing tall and alert. Her mere presence gave me a sense of security and reassurance. It's moments like these that remind me of the incredible bond we share."

Martha, a long-time Bullmastiff owner, shares her insights: "Having owned Bullmastiffs for many years,

I've come to appreciate their unique characteristics. Their calm and patient nature makes them wonderful with children, and they quickly become the family's gentle giant. Bullmastiffs have a way of sensing emotions and providing comfort during difficult times. Their intuitive nature and unwavering loyalty make them truly special companions."

These stories from Bullmastiff owners highlight the exceptional qualities of the breed. From their protective instincts to their gentle nature, Bullmastiffs have a remarkable impact on the lives of their owners. They bring joy, love, and a sense of security that is unparalleled.

It's important to note that every Bullmastiff has their own unique personality and experiences. Each owner's journey with their Bullmastiff is special and filled with memorable moments. Whether it's the heartwarming cuddles, the playful antics, or the unwavering loyalty, Bullmastiffs have a way of leaving a lasting impression on their owners' lives.
If you're considering adding a Bullmastiff to your family, take comfort in knowing that you'll be joining a community of passionate and supportive owners.

Connecting with other Bullmastiff enthusiasts can provide valuable advice, share experiences, and foster lifelong friendships. Online forums, social media groups, and local breed clubs are great places to start. By listening to the stories and experiences of Bullmastiff owners, you'll gain a deeper appreciation for the breed and understand the joys and challenges that come with owning a Bullmastiff.

Each story serves as a reminder of the incredible bond and love that can be forged between humans and their Bullmastiffs. Prepare to embark on a journey filled with laughter, love, and treasured memories as you welcome a Bullmastiff into your life.

Saying Goodbye: Dealing with Loss and Grief

Saying goodbye to a beloved Bullmastiff can be one of the most challenging and heartbreaking experiences for any owner. These gentle giants become cherished members of our families, and their loss leaves a void that is deeply felt. In this section, we'll discuss how to navigate the difficult journey of saying goodbye and coping with the grief that follows.

When the time comes to say goodbye to your Bullmastiff, it's important to remember that you provided them with a loving and fulfilling life. Reflect on the incredible memories and the joy your Bullmastiff brought into your life. Celebrate their unique personality, their unwavering loyalty, and the special bond you shared.

Grieving the loss of a Bullmastiff is a personal and individual process. It's natural to experience a range of emotions, from sadness and heartache to anger and guilt. Allow yourself to feel these emotions and give yourself the time and space needed to heal. Surround yourself with a support system of friends, family, and fellow Bullmastiff owners who can understand and empathize with your grief.

Some owners find comfort in creating a memorial for their Bullmastiff. This can be as simple as displaying their photo, setting up a special corner with their favorite toys and belongings, or planting a tree or flowers in their memory. These acts of remembrance can provide a sense of closeness and honor the bond you shared.

If you find it difficult to cope with the loss on your own, consider seeking professional support. Grief counseling or support groups can provide a safe space to share your feelings and find solace in the stories of others who have gone through similar experiences. Talking openly about your emotions and sharing memories of your Bullmastiff can be therapeutic and help in the healing process.

Remember that healing takes time, and there is no right or wrong way to grieve. Allow yourself to grieve at your own pace and in your own way. Some owners choose to honor their Bullmastiff's memory by welcoming a new furry companion into their lives when they are ready, while others prefer to take their time before considering another pet. Only you can determine what feels right for you.

As time passes, the pain of loss will gradually give way to cherished memories and a deep appreciation for the love and companionship you shared with your Bullmastiff. Their spirit will always live on in your heart, and the lessons they taught you about love, loyalty, and resilience will forever shape your life.

In the journey of life with a Bullmastiff, saying goodbye is an inevitable part, but it doesn't diminish the impact they had on your life. Treasure the memories, honor their legacy, and know that your Bullmastiff's love will remain with you forever. Take comfort in knowing that your beloved Bullmastiff lived a life filled with love, happiness, and the best care possible under your guidance.

Saying goodbye to a Bullmastiff is never easy, but in time, you'll find solace in the cherished memories and the enduring bond you shared. Allow yourself to grieve, seek support, and hold onto the love that will forever connect you and your Bullmastiff. They may be physically gone, but their spirit will always be by your side, guiding you with their gentle presence and unconditional love.

CONCLUSION: IS A BULLMASTIFF RIGHT FOR YOU?

Throughout this book, we have explored the various aspects of owning a Bullmastiff, from their history and characteristics to their care, training, and the joys and challenges of life with these magnificent dogs. As we conclude our journey, it's important to reflect on whether a Bullmastiff is the right fit for you and your lifestyle.

Bullmastiffs are truly special dogs, known for their gentle nature, loyalty, and protective instincts. They can make wonderful companions and devoted family pets for the right owner. However, it's crucial to consider several factors before bringing a Bullmastiff into your life.

First and foremost, Bullmastiffs are a large and powerful breed. They require ample space to move around comfortably and a secure and well-fenced yard to ensure their safety. Their size also means they need regular exercise to keep them physically and mentally stimulated. If you have an active lifestyle and enjoy outdoor activities, a Bullmastiff could be a great fit for you.

Another important aspect to consider is the amount of time and effort you are willing to invest in their care and training. Bullmastiffs require consistent socialization and training from an early age to ensure they grow up to be well-behaved and obedient dogs. They thrive on positive reinforcement and need a patient and committed owner who is willing to dedicate time and effort to their development.

Additionally, Bullmastiffs have specific grooming needs. Their short coats require regular brushing to keep them clean and free from loose hair. They are moderate shedders, so be prepared for some regular vacuuming. They also have specific health considerations, such as potential hip and elbow dysplasia, so regular veterinary check-ups and a nutritious diet are essential.

Financially, owning a Bullmastiff can be a significant commitment. From purchasing a puppy from a reputable breeder to providing proper nutrition, regular veterinary care, and grooming supplies, it's important to be prepared for the financial responsibilities that come with owning a large breed.

Furthermore, it's crucial to assess whether a Bullmastiff aligns with your lifestyle and living situation. They are typically calm and gentle indoors, making them suitable for apartment living as long as they have sufficient exercise and mental stimulation. However, their size and protective instincts mean they require responsible ownership and may not be suitable for households with very young children or other small pets.

Ultimately, the decision to bring a Bullmastiff into your life should be based on careful consideration of all these factors. They are loyal and loving companions that can bring immense joy and happiness to your household. However, it's essential to ensure that you have the time, resources, and commitment to meet their needs and provide them with a loving and suitable home.

If you are ready to embrace the responsibilities and rewards of owning a Bullmastiff, you will be rewarded with a lifetime of unconditional love, loyalty, and companionship. The bond you form with a Bullmastiff can be truly extraordinary, and they will forever hold a special place in your heart.

In conclusion, a Bullmastiff may be the right choice for you if you have the space, time, and dedication to meet their needs. They are gentle giants with a kind and protective nature, making them excellent family pets for those who understand and appreciate their unique qualities. However, it's essential to do your research, engage with reputable breeders, and ensure you are fully prepared to provide the love, care, and attention that a Bullmastiff deserves.

We hope this book has provided you with valuable insights and information to help you make an informed decision. Remember, owning a Bullmastiff is a lifelong commitment, and with the right preparation and care, you can embark on a beautiful journey filled with unconditional love and cherished memories with your Bullmastiff companion.

ABOUT THE AUTHOR

Rui Navarro is a seasoned and passionate dog owner, breeder, and trainer who has dedicated many years of his life to the field of canine behavior, health, and genetics. His passion for dogs and their well-being has led him to become one of the leading experts in the field, providing expert guidance and advice to fellow dog owners, breeders, and trainers.

With a deep understanding of the needs and concerns of dog owners, Rui has dedicated his career to providing practical and effective solutions to help them achieve their goals and succeed in the world of dog breeding. Throughout his journey, he has developed a wealth of knowledge and expertise that he is eager to share with others.

Rui's dedication to the world of dogs is evident in his commitment to helping others achieve their goals and in his unwavering passion for the well-being of our furry friends. Whether you are a first-time dog owner or a seasoned pro, Rui's expertise and guidance will be invaluable in helping you provide the best possible care for your dog.

THE BULLMASTIFF

Printed in Great Britain
by Amazon

36641085R00145